Miguel Ángel Almarza
Tania Bastow
Vincent A. Desmond
Jose Miguel Galarza
Jon Hird
Ceri Jones
Pascual Pérez Paredes
Ruth Sánchez García
Carmen Santos Maldonado
Nicholas Sheard
Russell Stannard

Inside Out

Resource Pack

Intermediate

Macmillan Heinemann English Language Teaching
Between Towns Road, Oxford OX4 3PP, UK
A division of Macmillan Publishers Limited
Companies and representatives throughout the world

ISBN 0 333 75759 9

Text © Sue Kay and Vaughan Jones 2000
Design and illustration © Macmillan Publishers Limited 2000
Heinemann is a registered trademark of Reed Educational and Professional Publishing Limited

First published 2000

Permission to copy

The material in this book is copyright. However, the publisher grants permission for copies to be made without fee on those pages marked with the PHOTOCOPIABLE symbol.

Private purchasers may make copies for their own use or for use by classes of which they are in charge; school purchasers may make copies for use, within and by the staff and students of the school only. This permission does not extend to additional schools or branches of an institution, who should purchase a separate master copy of the book for their own use.

For copying in any other circumstances, prior permission in writing must be obtained from Macmillan Publishers Limited.

Designed by Sarah Nicholson
Illustrated by Peter Cambell pp6a, 11c; Celia Canning pp1b, 3c, 4b, 6c; Paul Collicut p1a; Rebecca Halls pp7a, 13c; Tim Kahane pp2a, 4c, 7b; Pauline King p9c; Colin Meir pp8a, 9b, 12a; Gary Rees pp4a, 6b.
Cover design by Andrew Oliver
Cover illustration © Howard Hodgkin

The authors and publishers would like to thank the following for permission to reproduce their material:
Rosemary A. Thurber and The Barbara Hogenson Agency for the story 'The Bear Who Could Let It Alone' from the book *Fables for Our Time* by James Thurber. Copyright © 1940 by James Thurber. Copyright renewed by Helen Thurber and Rosemary A. Thurber.

Whilst every effort has been made to locate the owners of copyright, in some cases this has been unsuccessful. The publishers apologise for any infringement or failure to acknowledge the original sources and will be glad to include any necessary correction in subsequent printings.

Cover printed in the UK by George Overs
Text printed and bound in the UK by Martins the Printers

2004
10 9 8 7

Introduction

This Resource Pack for teachers contains over 40 practice activities for intermediate students of English. It is designed to be used with Inside Out Intermediate Student's Book.

Eleven practising teachers have contributed activities, so you'll find a wealth of different ideas for practising skills and specific language points. All the activities have been tested in the classroom.

Using the worksheets

You can use the activities in many different ways. For example:
- to extend the lessons in the student's book
- as revision of points in the student's book, for example at the beginning of the following lesson
- to supplement other courses
- as a basis for standby lessons

How to use the resource pack

Each activity consists of one photocopiable worksheet original. The originals have been designed for maximum clarity when photocopied. However, if your photocopier has the facility to enlarge, you may sometimes find this useful – particularly for board games or worksheets which are to be cut up into cards.

Each original appears on the right-hand page, with teacher's notes on the left-hand page so that you can see them both at the same time. The notes explain the aims of the activity, describe the task, tell you what you need to do to prepare and then give a step by step lesson plan. This makes them easy to use if you haven't been teaching long, but it also is a terrific time-saver for experienced teachers. Regard the lesson plans as a starting point. As you use the worksheets you'll find your own ways of making the best of them in class. Some of the worksheets need cutting up into sections. To make these easier to handle in the classroom, glue them onto small pieces of card – index cards or blank business cards, available from most stationer's, are ideal. After the lesson, file the cards in an envelope for the next time you use them. Write the name of the activity and the number of cards on the outside.

Some activities require multiple sets of cards. In these cases, it is a good idea to distinguish each set in some way. Put a different mark, preferably in different coloured pens, on the cards from each set. Or, even better, photocopy them on different coloured papers. This will save you time when you re-file them at the end of the lesson.

Over to you

If you have any comments about Inside Out – suggestions, criticisms or even praise – send us an email at *insideoutmail@mhelt.com*. Alternatively, there's a feedback form on our website at *www.mhelt.com*. Your opinions will help to shape our future publishing.

If you're interested in writing worksheets for our photocopiable resource packs, let us know. Send an email to *authors@mhelt.com*. Tell us what you're interested in, for example, general or business English, or perhaps a particular level or type of worksheet. Include a brief outline of your experience and qualifications, but don't, at this stage, send any sample materials.

Contents

Worksheet	Timing (minutes)	Task	Aim (lexis, grammar, pronunciation, skills)
1A You in pictures	15–30	To choose images to represent the student's own character.	To activate and practise language related to personal characteristics.
1B Reasons to be famous	45	To role play an interview with a famous person. To write a short biographical article.	To practise basic question forms in the main tenses and with modals.
1C Questions, questions, questions	30	To find, write down and ask and answer questions.	To practise recognizing, answering and asking questions.
2A Blockbuster	45–60	To prepare an outline for a film using prompts from the worksheet.	To practise writing the outline of a narrative.
2B Crosswords	45	To write and exchange crossword clues.	To distinguish between -ed and -ing adjectives.
2C The stress test	30	To answer a questionnaire.	To practise vocabulary linked to the themes of stress and relaxation.
3A Love is …?	35	To talk about and grade different romantic situations.	To practise using adverbs of degree.
3B Irregular battleships	30–40	Spelling game	To practise the spelling of irregular verbs.
3C Parents' day	40–50	To simulate a parents' visiting day at a school.	To practise being tactful.
4A Moments in American history	10–15	To ask and answer questions about past events.	To practise the difference between the past simple and past continuous.
4B Guess the sport	20–25	To guess the correct sport by asking questions.	To practise vocabulary related to sports and sporting events. To practise yes/no questions and short answers.
4C A windfall	15–20	Active dictation.	To practise listening for key words in a narrative and using them to re-tell the story.
5A Clueless	30	To complete a crossword.	To practise defining clauses.
5B School jokes	15–20	To match two halves of a joke.	To practise listening and speaking in a humorous context.
5C When I was at school …	30	To talk about schooldays and experiences related to that time.	To practise defining relative clauses within the communicative context of 'education'.
6A A true crime story	25–30	To re-tell a story.	To practise crime vocabulary.
6B Making news	30–40	To put together and tell a story, using picture cards.	To practise forms of the past tense verbs (both regular and irregular).
6C Hi! How are you?	20–40	To mime events.	To practise using the present perfect for news events.
7A The dinner party	45	To choose guests for a dinner party, devise a seating plan and write a menu for them.	To practise expressing opinions and vocabulary of food.
7B Fiesta	40–50	To present information to a committee to bid for a contract for the organization of a school trip. To discuss and decide on the best bid.	To practise presenting information, discussing and decision-making.
8A True or false?	20–30	To make a list of true and false statements.	To practise tenses and aspects.
8B Dominoes	15–20	To complete sentences using word dominoes.	To practise prepositions.
8C Phonetics guessing	40–50	Vocabulary guessing.	To practise the recognition of sounds and phonetic symbols.

Worksheet	Timing (minutes)	Task	Aim (lexis, grammar, pronunciation, skills)
9A *By the year 10,000*	20	To produce a class survey of predictions about the future.	To practise using *will* for predictions.
9B *Interpreter*	30	To simulate an act of communication between two people that speak different languages with the help of an interpreter.	To practise reported speech.
9C *The wedding*	40	To act out a dialogue.	To practise the sound /ə/ in connected speech.
10A *How well organized are you?*	about 20	To complete a questionnaire about personal organization and time management.	To practise lexis relating to time and personal organization.
10B *Rules and regulations*	30–40	To write a set of rules and regulations (obligation, permission, prohibition and no obligation) that apply to a given place.	To practise using modals of obligation and permission. To practise paraphrasing.
10C *Detectives*	20–30	To piece together a story using clues.	To practise time expressions/discussion.
11A *Useless information*	20	To exchange information.	To practise numbers.
11B *Postcards*	20	To complete two postcards – one sent from a bad holiday, one from a good holiday.	To enable learners to practise the language of describing places, travel and geographical location.
11C *Globetrotters*	30	To choose the best candidate for an award.	To practise the present perfect.
12A *Lies and statistics*	30	To determine which facts are true, and which are false. Sentence auction.	To practise speaking and listening.
12B *Food, sleep and shelter*	15	To put words in the correct category.	To revise and reinforce vocabulary from Unit 12 in Inside Out Student's Book.
12C *Just a minute!*	20–30	To fill in a grid with countable and uncountable nouns.	To practise countable and uncountable nouns.
13A *Know-it-alls*	20	To prepare and ask questions about other students' areas of knowledge.	To practise asking and answering questions.
13B *Make & do*	15–20	To mime an action involving a *make* or *do* expression for other students to guess.	To revise and practise collocations of *make* and *do*.
13C *Feng Shui*	30	To follow instructions to furnish an office according to the rules of Feng Shui.	To review and practise various structures, including conditionals.
14A *Dress to kill*	20	To decide how someone should dress for a job interview.	To practise descriptions and vocabulary of clothes.
14B *First impressions*	about 20	To agree on a list of do's and don'ts for an interview.	To practise talking about clothes and personal appearance, giving advice, negotiating, expressing opinions.
15A *If ...*	20	To create a chain of conditional sentences.	To practise using conditionals.
15B *I wish*	20	To complete wishes and guess who wrote them.	To practise the *I wish ...* structure.
15C *Then and now*	40–45	To exchange and compare personal information about the past and the present.	To practise asking and answering questions.
16A *How well do you know your classmates?*	20	To guess the answers to questions about your classmates and check whether or not you are correct.	To practise question forms.
16B *The bear who could let it alone*	15	To read a story and replace symbols with the words they stand for.	To consolidate basic uses of prepositions and conjunctions.

TEACHER'S NOTES

1A *You in pictures*

Jon Hird

Type of activity
Discussion. Pair and group work.

Aim
To activate and practise language related to personal characteristics.

Task
To choose images to represent the student's own character.

Preparation
Make one copy of the worksheet for each student. Take a few minutes to look at the pictures yourself. Think about what the pictures signify to you – although these interpretations may be different for everyone.

Timing
15–30 minutes

Procedure
1 Give each student a worksheet.
2 Ask the students to think about their own character and to choose the *five* images that best represent this. Then, tick or circle them.
3 Ask the students to complete the sentences at the bottom of the worksheet.
4 In pairs or small groups, the students explain their choices to each other.

Follow up
Hold a brief open class discussion of which images best represent the class as a whole. Encourage discussion of which characteristics each of the images could represent.

Notes & comments
For classes where the students know each other well, variations on stage 4 above are:
- Students guess their partner's choices before the discussion.
- With the writing at the bottom folded out of sight, the worksheets are collected and then randomly distributed. The students have to guess whose worksheet they have got before the discussion can take place.
- With the writing at the bottom folded out of sight, the worksheets are collected and then put on the walls of the classroom. The students walk around the room, in pairs or small groups, deciding whose is whose.

1A You in pictures

Look at the pictures below. Choose the five that best represent you.

The pictures that best represent me are …

… the _____ because _____ .
… the _____ because _____ .
… the _____ because _____ .
… the _____ because _____ .
… the _____ because _____ .

The pictures that best represent the class are _____
because _____ .

TEACHER'S NOTES

1B Reasons to be famous

Tania Bastow and Ceri Jones

Type of activity
Speaking and writing. Group work, pair work and individual work.

Aim
To practise basic question forms in the main tenses and with modals.

Task
To role play an interview with a famous person. To write a short biographical article.

Preparation
Make one or two copies (depending on class size) of the worksheet and cut them up into cards – a sentence and a picture on each card.

Timing
45 minutes

Procedure
1. Divide the class into two groups. Ask one group to brainstorm answers to the question: 'What are people famous for?' Ask the other group to brainstorm answers to the question: 'What information do people like to know about famous people?'
2. Ask the two groups to report back on their discussion.
3. Divide the students into pairs. Tell them that they have all suddenly become famous and give everyone a 'Reasons to be famous' card. (Use the blank cards if you need them. Students can write in their own 'Reasons to be famous'.) Allow a minute or two for students to check vocabulary – either with you or in dictionaries.
4. Explain that they are going to interview each other for a glossy magazine (like *Hello!*). Tell them that the person they are going to interview is incredibly busy and can only spare five minutes for the interview, and they need to find out as much interesting information as possible in the time given. After five minutes, tell the students to swap roles.
5. Ask the students to work individually and write the opening paragraph for their article. When they've finished, let them read each other's work.

Follow up
Ask students to bring in passport-size photographs of themselves, and the articles and photographs could be displayed on a 'Class Biographies' poster.

Notes & comments
This activity works well with classes who do not know each other very well and can be used as an extended icebreaker. It is also a good diagnostic activity at the beginning of a course.
Hello! is a popular British magazine that often has interviews with celebrities and photos of their houses and families.

1B Reasons to be famous

You are the mother/father of 12 children and next month you are expecting triplets.

You have just discovered you can read people's minds.

You are the invisible man/woman.

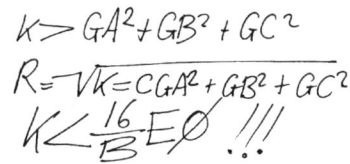
You were born in 2400 and are the inventor of time travel.

You saved the world from a computer-generated disaster.

You have just published your first novel and it is already a best-seller.

You have just flown around the world in a hot-air balloon.

You have just discovered a cure for the common cold.

You are the first person who has been on holiday to the moon.

Your name is Jonah. You have survived being swallowed by a whale.

You have just woken up after 20 years in a coma.

You won a record-breaking £25m on the lottery exactly a year ago today and you are giving your first interview to the press.

It is your 150th birthday. You are officially the oldest person on Earth.

You are the first extraterrestrial being to announce your arrival on Earth.

You have just got engaged to _____

You are _____
_____
_____
_____

You are _____
_____
_____
_____

You are _____
_____
_____
_____

TEACHER'S NOTES

1C Questions, questions, questions
Jon Hird

Type of activity
Reading, writing and speaking. Pair work.

Aim
To practise recognizing, answering and asking questions.

Task
To find, write down and then ask and answer questions.

Preparation
Make one copy of the worksheet for each student.

Timing
30 minutes

Procedure
1. Give out one worksheet for each student. Tell students to read through the answers and check the meanings of any words they don't understand, either with you or using dictionaries.
2. Working in pairs, the students have to find all the questions and write them next to the appropriate answers.
3. The students now take turns to ask each other these questions, writing down their partner's answers in the spaces on the worksheet. Encourage the students to ask follow-up questions to find out more information, e.g. 'What's your favourite city?' 'Madrid. And yours?' 'London.' 'Why London?'
4. Ask each student to report back three things they have learned about their partner.

Answers
Have you got a pet?
Where would you like to be right now?
Do you play a musical instrument?
Would you like to go to the moon?
Which country would you most like to visit?
How often do you speak English?
Who is your favourite singer?
Are you reading a book at the moment?
Could you speak English when you were ten?
What kind of music do you like?
How many countries have you been to?
Which is your favourite city?
Have you ever been to the UK?
Are you any good at cooking?
Have you got any children?
Can you count to ten in five languages?
How are you feeling right now?
Who chose your name?
What were you doing at midnight last night?
What is your favourite colour?

Follow up
The students can find out more about each other by asking further questions.

Notes & comments
A time limit can be imposed for stage 2 – say 10 minutes – with the pairs sharing their findings if they haven't found all the questions when this time has elapsed.

1C Questions, questions, questions

Find twenty questions and then write them next to their answers.

wherisholdwherowhichisyourfavouritecityhwothuldemwhetcanytwouldyouliketogoto
themoonsyouduifydoeahaveyougotanychildrenwitcthwhiydobilpsdoyouplayamusical
instrumentghieslhowhoinwasdoemycouldyouspeakanyenglishwhenyouwerenwhay
usetozdeoswheraedobwhochoseyournamewherdidyeuseghaveyougotapetaskiwherae
dwvdiwharecanyoucounttoteninfivelanguageshpdopleaswasawhatwereyoudoingatmi
dnightlastnightibegetwasiflwhatkindofmusicdoyoulikewerdothowareyoufeelingrightn
owhertowivuareyouanygoodatcookingdoesahxilwhichcountrywouldyoumostliketovis
itdifrilpareyoureadingabookatthemomentewhywhereacroapwhoisyourfavouritesinger
bitudoyooudidwathhowmanycountrieshaveyoubeentowhoiservizatwherewouldyouli
ketoberightnowofdoyudoyuolivatwhatisyourfavouritecolourhwomucthdoitothasyhav
eyoueverbeentotheukenwharhowoftendoyouspeakenglishereinomucthdoitothasyhav

Questions	Answers	Your partner's answers
_____?	A goldfish called Jimi.	_____.
_____?	On a beach in Thailand.	_____.
_____?	The banjo.	_____.
_____?	As long as I could come back.	_____.
_____?	Probably Mongolia.	_____.
_____?	Every day, usually.	_____.
_____?	Frank Sinatra.	_____.
_____?	No, not at the moment.	_____.
_____?	A little bit.	_____.
_____?	Country and Western, mainly.	_____.
_____?	Fifteen or so.	_____.
_____?	Delhi.	_____.
_____?	Yes, a couple of years ago.	_____.
_____?	Well, I can make an omelette.	_____.
_____?	Not yet.	_____.
_____?	No, only four.	_____.
_____?	A little tired, actually.	_____.
_____?	My mother, I think.	_____.
_____?	Getting ready for bed.	_____.
_____?	Purple.	_____.

TEACHER'S NOTES

2A Blockbuster

Nicholas Sheard

Type of activity
Speaking, writing. Pair work and group work.

Aim
To practise writing the outline of a narrative.

Task
To prepare an outline for a film using prompts from the worksheet.

Preparation
Make one copy of the worksheet for each group of three or four students.
Take a short video clip from a well-known film. (Optional)

Timing
45–60 minutes

Procedure
1 If you have a TV and video, play the first 3 minutes of a well-known film for the students. Otherwise, write the title of a film on the board (e.g. 'Star Wars'). Ask them what type of film it is (e.g. 'science fiction').
2 Brainstorm different categories/genres of film and write them on the board, e.g. *romance, adventure, drama, comedy, musical, western, thriller, horror, action, science fiction, animation, documentary*. Elicit films the students have seen in each of the categories.
3 Divide the students into groups of three or four.
4 Tell them they are going to write an outline for a film. The group with the best outline will get (a notional) $100 million to make their movie.
5 Give each group a copy of the worksheet. Ask them to choose at least three items from each column.
6 The groups build up the details of a plot, using their chosen location, characters, props and events. Set a time limit. Circulate and help them with vocabulary and ideas as necessary. Each group also thinks of three possible titles for their movie and chooses the actors and actresses to appear in their film.
7 Each group, in turn, presents its outline to the rest of the class. The class then decides which of the three titles is the best for the movie that has been described.
8 After the presentations, the class votes for the best idea (they can't vote for their own) and a winner is declared.

Follow up
Students write a scene from their film with dialogue. They then rehearse and act out the scene (this could be filmed if your school has a video camera).

Notes & comments
As an alternative for larger classes: each group invents one title for their movie and gives it to the teacher, who writes up all the titles on the board. The class listens to the presentations and guesses which title was written for each film outline.

2A *Blockbuster*

Choose at least three items from each column.

Location	Characters	Props	Events
A haunted house	A robot	A sword	An explosion
A museum	A model	A gun	A chase
A church	An inventor	A book	A party
A spaceship	A baby	Poison	A festival
A desert	A cowboy	A diamond	A trial
Australia	A soldier	A code	A race
Antarctica	A doctor	A bomb	A competition
Mars	An explorer	A key	An investigation
A farmhouse	A politician	A password	A fight
A swimming pool	A monster	A picture	A battle
A school	A giant	A clue	A discovery
A hotel	A cook	A maze	A phone call
A theatre	A policeman	A magic lamp	A test

> TEACHER'S NOTES

2B Crosswords

Tania Bastow and Ceri Jones

Type of activity
Writing. Group work.

Aim
To distinguish between *-ed* and *-ing* adjectives.

Task
To write and exchange crossword clues.

Preparation
Make one copy of the worksheet for every two students and cut it into four as indicated.

Timing
45 minutes

Procedure
1 Divide the class into two groups: group A and group B. Explain that they are going to write crossword clues for each other.
2 Give each member of group A a copy of 'Crossword A: the solution'.
Give each member of group B a copy of 'Crossword B: the solution'.
3 Allow them a few minutes to check on any words they are unsure of, either with you or in their dictionaries.
4 Within each group put the students in pairs.
5 Ask the pairs to write a crossword clue for each word. Students should not write their clues on the crossword solution.
6 Circulate and monitor, helping with vocabulary and any other problems.
7 When they have completed the clues, take the clues from the pairs in group A, and give them to the pairs in group B, with the appropriate crossword and vice versa.
8 If students are having difficulties with any of the clues encourage them to look at the clues of the other students in their group.
9 When they have finished, let them check the solutions.

Notes & comments
Some of the solutions are the same for both crosswords. Let the students find this out for themselves when they come to filling in the grids.

2B Crosswords

Crossword A

Crossword A: the solution

Across
2 trained
6 stressed
7 amused
8 addicted
9 engaged

Down
1 amusing
3 reassuring
4 interested
5 daring

Crossword B

Crossword B: the solution

Across
3 tiring
4 relaxed
7 scared
8 addicted
9 daring

Down
1 stressed
2 interested
5 amazing
6 moved

TEACHER'S NOTES

2C *The stress test*

Tania Bastow and Ceri Jones

Type of activity
Reading and speaking. Pair work.

Aim
To practise vocabulary linked to the themes of stress and relaxation.

Task
To answer a questionnaire.

Preparation
Make copies of 'The Stress Test – Part One' and 'The Stress Test – Part Two' and cut them so that there is one copy for every pair of students.

Timing
30 minutes

Procedure

1 Divide the students into pairs. Tell them they're going to complete a stress test but before they do so they have to give their partner a stress rating from 1 (relaxed) to 10 (highly stressed).

2 Give each student A a copy of 'The Stress Test – Part One' and each student B a copy of 'The Stress Test – Part Two'.

3 Ask the students to read their questionnaires and make a note of their answers. They can do this on the test sheet or on a separate sheet of paper.

4 Ask the pairs of students to ask each other the questions in their part of the test. They should read out the questions rather than let their partner read them from the sheet.

5 Circulate, helping with vocabulary.

6 As the pairs finish both parts of the test, give them a copy of the key below to work out their results.

7 Ask students to comment on their results and compare them to the rating they were given at the beginning of the exercise.

Key

1	a 3	b 1	c 0	d 1
2	a 2	b 1	c 3	d 0
3	a 2	b 3	c 2	d 0
4	a 1	b 2	c 0	d 2
5	a 3	b 2	c 1	d 0
6	a 2	b 2	c 0	d 1
7	a 1	b 1	c 0	d 3
8	a 1	b 0	c 1	d 2
9	a 3	b 1	c 2	d 1
10	a 0	b 3	c 1	d 2
11	a 3	b 0	c 1	d 1
12	a 3	b 2	c 1	d 0

If you scored 26–33, you're heading for a crisis. Lighten up. Try to relax and enjoy life more. Take a holiday.

If you scored 18–25, you're probably worrying too much. Solve your problems or forget about them.

If you scored 8–17, you're dealing with life well and enjoying it. Be understanding with people who find it harder to relax than you do.

If you scored 0–7, you don't have enough stress. Maybe you haven't noticed something. Take a look around. Nobody's life is that easy.

Follow up
Ask the students to give each other advice on how to reduce their stress levels.

2C *The stress test*

THE STRESS TEST – PART ONE
Are you stressed out? Answer this quiz and find out!

1. How many hours have you slept in the last 3 days?
   - a less than 15 hours
   - b between 15 and 18
   - c between 18 and 24
   - d over 24 hours

2. When was the last time you really laughed?
   - a on my last holiday
   - b sometime in the last week
   - c I can't remember
   - d today

3. How many times have you lost your temper in the last two days?
   - a I never lose my temper
   - b I've lost count
   - c once or twice
   - d I haven't in the last couple of days but I do occasionally

4. When you get angry with someone do you
   - a shout at them?
   - b ignore them?
   - c explain why you are angry?
   - d complain to someone else?

5. How many of the following things did you do last weekend?
   – saw friends or family
   – did something you really enjoy
   – spent some time outside
   - a none of them   c 2
   - b 1   d all 3

6. How often do you do a sport?
   - a I don't like doing sport
   - b only on the beach in the summer
   - c two or three times a week
   - d at the weekend

THE STRESS TEST – PART TWO
Are you stressed out? Answer this quiz and find out!

7. How often do you diet?
   - a never
   - b I start a diet every Monday
   - c when I've put on a couple of kilos
   - d I'm always on a diet

8. How many caffeine-rich drinks (coffee, tea, Coca-Cola) do you drink a day?
   - a never
   - b only in the morning
   - c at least three or four
   - d it depends on how many I need to keep me awake

9. When you're stressed which of the following do you do?
   – smoke
   – eat comfort food
   – drink alcohol
   - a all of them
   - b none, I do something else
   - c none, I try not to react
   - d one or two

10. Which of the following make you feel particularly stressed?
    – waiting in a long queue
    – arguing with people
    – people who are always late
    – inefficiency
    - a none of them
    - b all of them
    - c one or two
    - d three of them

11. How often do you feel you have too little time?
    - a every day
    - b never
    - c occasionally
    - d just before a deadline or an exam

12. Which of these best applies to you?
    - a I worry about everything
    - b I worry about something at some time almost every day
    - c I worry when things are worth worrying about
    - d I never worry

THE STRESS TEST – HOW DID YOU SCORE?
So, are you stressed out? Add up your score and find out!

1	a 3	b 1	c 0	d 1	7	a 1	b 1	c 0	d 3
2	a 2	b 1	c 3	d 0	8	a 1	b 0	c 1	d 2
3	a 2	b 3	c 2	d 0	9	a 3	b 1	c 2	d 1
4	a 1	b 2	c 0	d 2	10	a 0	b 3	c 1	d 2
5	a 3	b 2	c 1	d 0	11	a 3	b 0	c 1	d 1
6	a 2	b 2	c 0	d 1	12	a 3	b 2	c 1	d 0

TEACHER'S NOTES

3A Love is ...?

Nicholas Sheard

Type of activity
Speaking. Pair work and group work.

Aim
To practise using adverbs of degree.

Task
To talk about and grade different romantic situations.

Preparation
Make one copy of the worksheet for each student.

Timing
35 minutes

Procedure

1. Draw a picture of a romantic situation on the board, e.g. two people having a meal with candles and roses on the table, or bring in a picture from a magazine. If you like, play a cassette of romantic music. Write *Love is ...?* on the board. Ask the students to suggest ways of completing the sentence.

2. Give one copy of the worksheet to each student and ask them to read through the twelve situations. Ask them to choose the most romantic situation. Circulate, helping with vocabulary.

3. After 5 minutes ask the students to stop reading and form pairs.

4. Explain that each pair is going to discuss how romantic the remaining situations are and grade them using hearts (5 hearts is extremely romantic, 1 heart is only slightly romantic). Explain that the students in each pair do not have to give the same grading.

5. Circulate, encouraging discussion and/or helping the pairs with vocabulary where necessary.

6. When most of the pairs have finished grading, bring the language at the bottom of the worksheet to their attention. Model and drill for pronunciation. Show how the structure changes for 'not really' and 'not at all'. Go through the results with the whole class, encouraging the students to use the adverbs of degree.

7. Ask the students to form new groups of four, each pair joining with another pair of similar opinion. Explain to the new groups that they are going to collaborate to produce another romantic situation. This time, they must agree on one new romantic situation.

8. When all the groups have completed their situation, discuss each one as a whole class, and ask the other groups to grade them by giving each situation a number of hearts. Again, encourage the students to use the adverbs of degree.

Follow up
Ask the students to conduct a class or school survey on what makes a romantic situation. The results could be presented in the form of a wall-chart or display.

Notes & comments
You could briefly brainstorm the language for agreement and disagreement at stage 4.

3A Love is …?

		You	Your partner
1	A candlelit dinner for two at home with romantic music and a log fire.	_____	_____
2	Champagne with strawberries and cream on a summer picnic in the countryside.	_____	_____
3	A kiss and a cuddle in front of the TV on a Friday night.	_____	_____
4	A violin playing for you under the bedroom window.	_____	_____
5	A stranger stopping you in the street with a bouquet of flowers.	_____	_____
6	A couple of 86 and 87 celebrating their diamond wedding anniversary.	_____	_____
7	A surprise weekend for two in a 4-star hotel in Paris/Venice/Prague.	_____	_____
8	A card and chocolates on Valentine's Day.	_____	_____
9	A moonlit swim.	_____	_____
10	Saying 'I love you' regularly.	_____	_____
11	Being ill together.	_____	_____
12	A marriage proposal on a cold, wet, windy walk in the countryside.	_____	_____

I think _____ is   extremely / very / quite   romantic

because _____ .

I don't think _____ is   really / at all   romantic

because _____ .

TEACHER'S NOTES

3B *Irregular battleships*
Ruth Sánchez García

Type of activity
Spelling, speaking. Pair work.

Aim
To practise the spelling of irregular verbs.

Task
Spelling game.

Preparation
Make one copy of the worksheet for every two students and cut them in two as indicated.

Timing
30–40 minutes

Procedure
1 Ask if any of the students have played the game 'Battleships'. If anyone has, ask them to explain it to the rest of the class.
2 Ask the students to form pairs of Student As and Student Bs.
3 Give each student a copy of the relevant worksheet.
4 Tell the students that the object of the game is to find ten irregular verbs in the past tense and past participle in their partner's grid.
5 Ask the students to read the instructions on their worksheets carefully. You may want to pre-teach some of the key lexis: *a grid, to score a hit, to miss, your turn, your go.*
6 Circulate, checking that students spell the verbs correctly.

Answers
The verbs on Worksheet A are: grew, stolen, won, led, put, heard, gone, ate, thrown, drove.
The verbs on Worksheet B are: sung, drunk, made, built, sat, hurt, woke, swam, cut, taught.

Follow up
- Ask the students to make a list with the infinitive, past tense and past participle forms of the twenty verbs that they have found.
- Use the blank grids below to play the game again: students can write in their own verbs. The grids can also be used for other lexical fields.

Notes & comments
For lower level classes, if you think it will take too long for the students to find out the verbs, write the twenty verbs on the blackboard before starting the game.

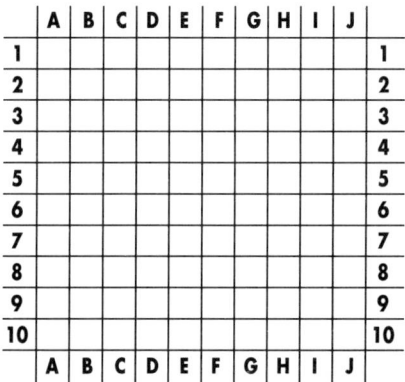

3B *Irregular battleships*

Worksheet A

In the first grid on your worksheet there are ten irregular verbs. They are all in the past tense or the past participle. They are written forwards, backwards, upwards or downwards, but not diagonally.

Your partner has to find your verbs without seeing your worksheet and you have to find ten verbs in your partner's worksheet.

Play the game by taking turns to call out grid references, for example A1, C5, G3 etc. When you name a square your partner has to tell you what's in it.

The winner is the first to find all the other verbs in his or her partner's worksheet.

	A	B	C	D	E	F	G	H	I	J	
1	W		N				G	R	E	W	1
2	O		E								2
3	N		L	D							3
4			O	E		P	U	T			4
5	N		T	L							5
6	W		S		D	R	O	V	E		6
7	O										7
8	R			D	R	A	E	H			8
9	H										9
10	T		G	O	N	E		E	T	A	10
	A	B	C	D	E	F	G	H	I	J	

	A	B	C	D	E	F	G	H	I	J	
1											1
2											2
3											3
4											4
5											5
6											6
7											7
8											8
9											9
10											10
	A	B	C	D	E	F	G	H	I	J	

Worksheet B

In the first grid on your worksheet there are ten irregular verbs. They are all in the past tense or the past participle. They are written forwards, backwards, upwards or downwards, but not diagonally.

Your partner has to find your verbs without seeing your worksheet and you have to find ten verbs in your partner's worksheet.

Play the game by taking turns to call out grid references, for example A1, C5, G3 etc. When you name a square your partner has to tell you what's in it.

The winner is the first to find all the other verbs in his or her partner's worksheet.

	A	B	C	D	E	F	G	H	I	J	
1	G	N	U	S		T	R	U	H		1
2											2
3	T		M		W	O	K	E			3
4	L		A								4
5	I		D		K	N	U	R	D		5
6	U		E						C		6
7	B			M	A	W	S		U		7
8		S							T		8
9		A									9
10		T			T	H	G	U	A	T	10
	A	B	C	D	E	F	G	H	I	J	

	A	B	C	D	E	F	G	H	I	J	
1											1
2											2
3											3
4											4
5											5
6											6
7											7
8											8
9											9
10											10
	A	B	C	D	E	F	G	H	I	J	

© Sue Kay & Vaughan Jones, 2000. Published by Macmillan Publishers Limited. This sheet may be photocopied and used within the class.

> TEACHER'S NOTES

3C Parents' day

Vincent A. Desmond

Type of activity
Speaking. Group or pair work.

Aim
To practise being tactful.

Task
To simulate a parents' visiting day at a school.

Preparation
Make one copy of the worksheet for each group or pair.

Timing
40–50 minutes

Procedure

1 Introduce the idea of parents' day (i.e. that parents visit the school and ask the different teachers how their children are doing).

2 Divide the class into pairs or groups. Hand out one set of pictures to each pair or group and put the following subjects on the board: art, maths, science, computers, English, sport. Ask the students to use the 'useful language' (+ any of their own) to describe each pupil from their appearance in the pictures (e.g. *Karen is very good at maths, quite popular, very hard-working, she likes science*, etc.). Note that students may need help with the qualifying adverbs (e.g. 'very nice' is possible, but 'absolutely nice' is not).

3 Compare the ideas of each pair/group.

4 Introduce the idea of the 'nice/tactful' teacher and the 'strict/tactless' teacher. Elicit how each would describe one of the students. For example:

Tactful:	Tactless:
Matthew **tends to be** late.	Matthew is always late.
Matthew **can be a bit** quiet at times.	Matthew is boring.
Matthew **is not particularly/ exactly** talkative.	Matthew never talks.

5 Divide the students into two equal groups: one group of parents (allocate one pupil picture to each parent) and one group of teachers (teachers decide if they are tactful or tactless). Move the teachers to different areas of the room. Parents then visit each teacher and get a report on their son or daughter (teachers give information about all subjects – they can say whatever they choose about any students).

6 After finishing, ask the parents which teachers were tactful and which were tactless and why.

INSIDE OUT Resource Pack

3C Parents' day

| Karen | Roger | Jeremy | Dorothy | Glen |
| Philip | David | Jane | Matthew | Helen |

Useful words and phrases:

can be ... tends to be ... isn't exactly ... isn't particularly	hard-working confident fit talkative selfish strong average ambitious self-centred	kind terrible naughty creative late weak aggressive slow big-headed	clever nice lovely overconfident lazy competitive absent-minded stupid over-sensitive
absolutely really very quite a bit not very not at all	interested in _____ ing good/excellent at _____ ing bad/awful at _____ ing		

© Sue Kay & Vaughan Jones, 2000. Published by Macmillan Publishers Limited. This sheet may be photocopied and used within the class.

Photocopiable

TEACHER'S NOTES

4A Moments in American history
Russell Stannard

Type of activity
Listening and speaking. Pair work.

Aim
To practise the difference between the past simple and past continuous.

Task
To ask and answer questions about past events.

Preparation
Make enough photocopies of worksheets A and B for each pair in the class.

Timing
10–15 minutes

Procedure
1. Tell students that they are going to practise the difference between the past simple and the past continuous.
2. Ask students to form pairs of Student As and Student Bs and give each student their corresponding sheet.
3. Allow a minute for students to look at their sheets. Explain to them that they have information about the Walton family and what different members were doing at different moments in the history of America.
4. Do an example with a student in the class so that students know what they have to do, e.g.:

   Student: What was Mrs Walton doing when Kennedy was assassinated?
   Teacher: She was cooking.

5. Suggest to students that they take it in turns to ask and answer questions. It is best to work across the page so that the students can substitute the names of the people for pronouns. For the You sections, ask them to use their imagination – and invent lies.

Notes & comments
It is well worth doing an example that includes the section 'You' so that the students understand what they are meant to do. You may want to elicit the question form before starting and write it up on the board. When students have got the idea, wipe it off the board.

INSIDE OUT *Resource Pack*

4A *Moments in American history*

Worksheet A

	October 29, 1929 ... the stock market crashed	December 8, 1941 ... the USA entered the Second World War	November 22, 1963 ... Kennedy was assassinated	July 20, 1969 ... the first man landed on the moon
Mr Walton	tour/France		relax	
Mrs Walton		iron		have
Junior Walton	rob		visit	
Grandpa Walton		drink		
You				

4A *Moments in American history*

Worksheet B

	October 29, 1929 ... the stock market crashed	December 8, 1941 ... the USA entered the Second World War	November 22, 1963 ... Kennedy was assassinated	July 20, 1969 ... the first man landed on the moon
Mr Walton		dance/nightclub		lie
Mrs Walton	wash		cook	
Junior Walton		attend		live
Grandpa Walton	drink		drink	
You				

© Sue Kay & Vaughan Jones, 2000. Published by Macmillan Publishers Limited. This sheet may be photocopied and used within the class.

Photocopiable

TEACHER'S NOTES

4B *Guess the sport*

Miguel Ángel Almarza

Type of activity
Speaking. Group work.

Aim
To practise vocabulary related to sports and sporting events.
To practise yes/no questions and short answers.

Task
To guess the correct sport by asking relevant yes/no questions.

Preparation
Make a copy of the worksheet for every four or five students. Cut up the worksheet as indicated.

Timing
20–25 minutes

Procedure

1 Tell the students you have a pack of cards. Each card has the name of a sport and some information about that sport on it.
2 Explain the rules of the game.
   - Students work in groups of four or five.
   - Each student in the group takes one card and reads it – without showing it to the others.
   - Students take turns to ask one yes/no question of any member of the group: *Is it a ball game? Do you play in teams?*
     They must nominate the person they want to ask: *My question is for Javier.*
   - The student answering the question should give short answers: *Yes, it is, No, you can't, I don't know, Sometimes, It depends ...*
   - Students can use their turn to make a guess (*Is it tennis?*). They may *only* guess during their turn. If the guess is right, the card holder drops out.
   - When only one student remains, the game is over and that student is the winner. Demonstrate the game if necessary.
3 Ask the students to form groups. Make sure that the seating arrangement allows them to listen to each other.
4 Give each group a set of cards facing down to be placed in the middle of the group. As they play the game, circulate and monitor.
5 When the first groups finish playing, get them to repeat the game with the remaining cards.

Follow up
Each group thinks of a sport and answers questions from other groups.

Notes & comments
As an alternative procedure, try telling the students that everybody has a starting score of 10 points: a wrong guess loses them 3 points and a correct guess earns them 3 points. Groups should keep their own written record of this. In this case, the winner is the student with the most points at the end.

4B Guess the sport

SQUASH
Individual sport; two players.
Equipment: small rubber ball and racket.
Place: indoor court.
Objective: to hit the ball so that the opponent misses it.
Very fast game. Requires a lot of stamina. You don't usually play for a long time.

BOXING
Individual sport. A fight between two people.
Equipment: big leather gloves.
Place: square ring.
Objective: to knock out or fight better than the opponent.
A fight is divided into 15 three-minute rounds.

SKIING
Individual sport.
Equipment: boots, skis and poles.
Place: outside. Snowy countryside, hills or mountains.
Objective: to move down hills or across the countryside in the snow.
In competition, skiers usually race against the clock.
It's a winter sport.

VOLLEYBALL
Team sport. 6 players in each team.
Equipment: a large leather ball and a high net.
Place: indoor or outdoor court.
Objective: to hit the ball back and forth over the net with your hands.
The first team to reach 15 points wins.

TABLE TENNIS
Individual or doubles sport.
Equipment: bat and small ball.
Place: table with a low net, usually indoors.
Objective: to hit the ball back and forth over the net.
Also called ping-pong. The first player to reach 21 wins.

SWIMMING
Individual sport or relay teams of 4.
Equipment: (optional) swimming cap and goggles.
Place: indoor or open air swimming-pools, rivers, lakes and the sea.
Objective: to move yourself through water as quickly as possible.
Strokes: crawl, breaststroke, backstroke and butterfly.

(FIELD) HOCKEY
Team sport. 11 players in each team.
Equipment: a stick and a ball.
Place: outdoor grass pitch.
Objective: to score goals.
Similar sports are played on ice or on roller-skates.

ICE-SKATING
Individual or couples, especially in figure skating.
Equipment: ice-skates.
Place: ice rink.
Objective: to move across ice on special boots with thin metal blades.
Speed and figure skating are the two main varieties.

WATER POLO
Team sport. Two teams of seven.
Equipment: ball, goalpost.
Place: swimming-pool.
Objective: to score goals.
You need to be a fast swimmer. It is played in 15-minute halves.

RUGBY
Team sport. 15 players in each team.
Equipment: oval ball.
Place: outdoor grass pitch.
Objective: to kick the ball between the two upright posts and over the crossbar or touch the ball down over the line. Matches are divided into two 40-minute halves.

> TEACHER'S NOTES

4C *A windfall*

Russell Stannard

Type of activity
Listening and speaking. Pair work.

Aim
To practise listening for key words in a narrative and using them to re-tell the story.

Task
Active dictation.

Preparation
Make a copy of the worksheet for each student and cut it in two as indicated.
Practise telling (or reading out) the story on the worksheet.

Timing
15–20 minutes

Procedure
1 Tell the students you are going to tell them a true story and that they should listen as carefully as possible but they cannot take notes.
2 Tell the story – or read it to them.
3 Divide the students into pairs.
4 Give one copy of the 'Connections' sheet to each pair.
5 Let them look at the words while you tell the story again.
6 Explain that they should take it in turns to connect two words together and explain why they have connected the two words. The connections must be related to the story, e.g.: *David and Taxi ... because David is a taxi driver.* Make sure students understand that they must explain why they have connected the two words.
7 Explain that when they have connected two words together they should cross them out and they cannot use these words again.
8 Circulate and monitor.
9 Stop the activity when students begin to find it difficult to think of connections. They don't have to connect them all.
10 Ask students to get into groups of four and get them to compare their connections, explaining why they made them. How many connections were the same?
11 Give them the story to read and to take away with them.

Follow up
By the end of stage 10 the students should be able to re-tell the whole story. Before giving them their own copy you could get them to re-tell the story collaboratively in their pairs or in groups.
For homework you could get the students to write the story or, working from the text, to paraphrase it, telling it in different words.

Notes & comments
If you have a big class, write the words on the board and get individual students to come up to the board and connect words. This way you have more control.

4C *A windfall*

One day, a few years ago, David Smith was working on his afternoon shift as a taxi driver. It was a warm day in August. On this particular day he was driving his black cab around the financial centre of London. He had stopped to buy a newspaper and was just getting back into his taxi when two men came running by. They were both wearing masks and had guns in their hands. They suddenly opened the doors of the taxi and told David to drive as fast as he could. The two men were incredibly nervous and one was shouting at the other. One of them was, in fact, so nervous that he was crying. David just drove, he didn't know what to do, he was completely frozen. Luckily, that part of London is not that busy on a Saturday and so they quickly got away from the scene of the crime. However, the two men continued to argue and shout at each other. They were both swearing and shouting and suddenly one of them punched the other and then jumped out of the taxi. The other one immediately got out and chased after him. David quickly drove away. He was feeling sick from being so nervous but he couldn't stop driving. He drove for at least 20 minutes until he felt safe. He then stopped the taxi and got out. He was sick on the side of the road from the nerves. When he got back in the taxi he noticed that the robbers had left the guns and a big black sack in the taxi.

David looked in the bag. It was stuffed with foreign currency. Dollars, German marks, French francs and Japanese yen. There was so much money in the bag that when David took the money home and started counting it, he got bored and never counted it all; he said he had counted for more than five hours but as the money was in different currencies it had got very complicated. There was even money from countries he didn't recognise.

David had little choice but to hand the money in because he was, of course, worried about the guns. However, he never received any compensation and the two men were never arrested. In a radio interview some years later he admitted that he regretted not keeping the money. He also confessed that his wife had wanted him to 'sit and wait and see what happens'. There was nearly one million pounds worth of used foreign currency.

Connections

to count   to cry   black sack
     to drive   to get out   to keep
to leave   to punch   to shout
     to shout   to swear   two robbers
wife   bored   compensation
     complicated   David Smith   five hours
     foreign currency   guns   money
newspaper   not busy   one million pounds
     regret   stop   taxi driver
to be interviewed   to be sick   to chase

TEACHER'S NOTES

5A Clueless

Tania Bastow and Ceri Jones

Type of activity
Mill drill. Whole class.

Aim
To practise defining clauses.

Task
To complete a crossword.

Preparation
Photocopy one set of the clues for each group of twelve students and cut them up. If there are fewer than twelve students in the class, either hand out one clue to each student and write in the solutions for the other clues on the grid, or give students more than one clue.
Make enough copies of the crossword grid for each student.

Timing
30 minutes

Procedure
1. Explain to the class that they are going to complete a crossword. Give each student a copy of the crossword and one or two clues.
2. Explain that they must help each other to complete the crossword. Before they start, they need to memorize their clues as they will be handing them back to you.
3. Allow a couple of minutes and then collect the clues back from the students.
4. Ask the students to stand up and mingle, exchanging clues and completing their crosswords. They should not show – or tell – each other any solutions.
5. Circulate, monitoring and helping with any problems.
6. When most of the students have finished, call an end to the activity.
7. Check the solutions with the whole class. Then ask them to re-write as many of the clues as they can remember.

Solutions

Across
2 toys
4 love
5 holidays
8 teenager
9 pram
10 zebra
11 soap

Down
1 playmate
3 smile
6 cereal
7 pupil
8 tears

5A Clueless

Ask other students for their clues to help you complete the crossword.

---

2 across
Things that are often given to children as gifts at Christmas or on their birthdays (4 letters)

4 across
A strong emotion which can change people's lives (4 letters)

5 across
The time of year that all schoolchildren (and their teachers) look forward to (8 letters)

8 across
A young person who is no longer a child but is not quite an adult either (8 letters)

9 across
A kind of cot or small bed on wheels which is used for taking babies out for a walk (4 letters)

10 across
A black and white African animal that shows us where to cross the road (5 letters)

11 across
A substance that you use with water for washing yourself or sometimes for washing clothes (4 letters)

1 down
A word which is used to describe a child's friend (8 letters)

3 down
One of the first forms of communication that a baby learns (5 letters)

6 down
A kind of food which is often eaten for breakfast with milk and sugar (6 letters)

7 down
A person, usually young, who is taught by another (5 letters)

8 down
Drops of salty water which come from the eye (5 letters)

TEACHER'S NOTES

5B *School jokes*

Pascual Pérez Paredes

Type of activity
Reading, listening and speaking. Mill drill.

Aim
To practise listening and speaking in a humorous context.

Task
To match two halves of a joke.

Preparation
Make enough copies of the cards on the worksheet and cut them up.

Timing
15–20 minutes

Procedure
1 Tell your students that they will each be given half of a joke: either the opening or the ending (punchline). You can use a well-known joke such as *Doctor, Doctor, everyone keeps ignoring me. – Next please!* to exemplify the kind of humour they can expect.
2 Give out the cards – one or more to each student, depending on class size. Allow a few minutes for students to check any vocabulary they don't know, either with you or in a dictionary.
3 Ask the students to walk around the classroom reading out their incomplete jokes to each other and deciding whether their halves match.
4 Ask the students to check with you when they think they have found their 'other half'.
5 When the activity is over, pairs read out their 'complete' jokes.

Solution
The jokes are:

I can still remember my university days ... – All three of them.

I'll never learn how to spell. – The teacher keeps changing the words.

What is black when clean and white when dirty? – A blackboard.

Where was the Declaration of Independence signed? – At the bottom.

One day I brought an apple for the teacher and she kissed me. – The next day I brought her a watermelon.

I spent three years in college taking medicine. – You poor thing. Are you well now?

It took me a whole year to write a book. – You idiot. Don't you know you can buy one for a fiver?

Before we begin this final exam, are there any questions? – Yes. What's the name of this course?

I want to read a book ... something very deep. – What about 20,000 Leagues Under the Sea?

So you flunked the history exam. – Yes. They kept asking questions about things that happened before I was born.

Now, class, are there any questions? – Yes. Where do those words go when you rub them off the blackboard?

What comes after six? – The milkman.

I got an A in spelling. – You fool. There isn't any A in 'spelling'.

Who needs a dictionary? – If you've read one you've read them all.

Notes & comments
The activity can also work as pair work. Cut the page in half: openings and endings. Students work in pairs to match the openings and endings by reading them aloud to each other.

5B School jokes

Openings	Endings
Before we begin this final exam, are there any questions?	The milkman.
I got an A in spelling.	Yes. They kept asking questions about things that happened before I was born.
Who needs a dictionary?	You fool. There isn't any A in 'spelling'.
I'll never learn how to spell.	Yes. Where do those words go when you rub them off the blackboard?
What is black when clean and white when dirty?	The teacher keeps changing the words.
Where was the Declaration of Independence signed?	You poor thing. Are you well now?
One day I brought an apple for the teacher and she kissed me.	If you've read one you've read them all.
I spent three years in college taking medicine.	Yes. What's the name of this course?
It took me a whole year to write a book.	What about 20,000 Leagues Under the Sea?
So you flunked the history exam.	You idiot. Don't you know you can buy one for a fiver?
Now, class, are there any questions?	At the bottom.
What comes after six?	All three of them.
I want to read a book … something very deep.	A blackboard.
I can still remember my university days …	The next day I brought her a watermelon.

TEACHER'S NOTES

5C When I was at school ...

Pascual Pérez Paredes

Type of activity
Speaking. Pair work.

Aim
To practise defining relative clauses within the communicative context of 'education'.

Task
To talk about schooldays and experiences related to that time.

Preparation
Make one copy of the worksheet for each pair of students. Each pair will need a coin.

Timing
30 minutes

Procedure
1 Introduce the topic of schooldays. Talk about your own. Pre-teach/check: *bully, teacher's pet, trouble-maker, subject*.
2 Divide the students into pairs.
3 Tell the students they will need a coin to play this game.
4 They toss the coin. If it is heads, they advance one square, if it is tails they advance two.
5 Student A tosses a coin and completes the statement on that square. Then, it's Student B's turn. If they can't complete the sentence, they miss the next turn.
6 The activity is finished when one student reaches the Finish square and completes the last sentence.

Follow up
Run a class debate about school.
Possible topics are:
- What makes a good school?
- What makes a good teacher?
- Schooldays are the best years in everyone's life.
- Friends are more important when you are a child.

Notes & comments
Not all statements include a relative clause.

5C When I was at school …

Start →

1. I knew a girl who …
2. I particularly used to enjoy subjects that …
3. I didn't like a schoolmate who …
4. There was a trouble-maker who …
5. There was a bully who …
6. There was a schoolmate who was punished for …
7. I had a very nice teacher who …
8. I remember an occasion when, in front of the whole group, I had to …
9. I didn't like lessons that …
10. I missed lessons when …
11. My least favourite subject was …
12. I always got … marks …
13. I had a very good teacher who …
14. My very best friend was a boy/girl who lived …
15. The teacher's pet was a boy/girl that …
16. I liked PE lessons in which …
17. I had a very strange schoolmate who …
18. My favourite subject was …
19. I had to get up …
20. There was a game that …
21. I liked a schoolboy/ schoolgirl who …

Finish

© Sue Kay & Vaughan Jones, 2000. Published by Macmillan Publishers Limited. This sheet may be photocopied and used within the class.

Photocopiable

TEACHER'S NOTES

6A A true crime story
Russell Stannard

Type of activity
Group work and story telling in pairs.

Aim
To practise crime vocabulary.

Task
To re-tell a story.

Preparation
Make a copy of the story for each group.

Timing
25–30 minutes

Procedure
1. Divide the class into two groups. Give one group story A and one group story B.
2. Tell the students to read their stories and make notes to remember them. A good way to help the students to remember their stories is to get each student in the group to prepare five comprehension questions about their story and then get them to read the questions to the rest of the group who then answer them. Move around the groups and help with vocabulary. (If you have a lot of students then make two groups of student As and two groups of student Bs.)
3. Regroup the students in pairs so that each pair has one student with story A and one student with story B.
4. Ask the students to tell their stories to their partners.
5. After both of them have told their stories they should make a list of the differences in their two stories.
6. Afterwards, get the pairs to explain the differences they found and you should list them on the board.
7. Tell them that one of the stories is true and the other is false. Take a vote – which one do they think is true? (The true story is the one set in Brazil.)

Answers

1. ... went on holiday to (A) Brazil, (B) America
2. ... for (A) a month, (B) two months
3. ... spent over (A) £1,000, (B) £1,200
4. ... had insured himself before going to (A) Brazil, (B) America
5. ... went to a rather dangerous part of (A) São Paulo, (B) New York
6. (A) ... he picked up a telephone and pretended to speak to someone, (B) ... he stood in front of a cigarette machine and bought a packet of cigarettes.
7. (A) ... across the road. He was now very nervous and ..., (B) ... across the road and he was nervous but ...
8. ... while (A) making a phone call, (B) buying a packet of cigarettes
9. (A) He was so nervous that even though the story wasn't true he started to cry. He gave a description of two men he had seen following him., (B) He told them he had lost a video camera, jewellery, money and clothes.
   He wasn't nervous at all. He had always liked acting and totally convinced the police.
10. ... every item over (A) £50, (B) £100
11. ... a telegram from the police in (A) Brazil, (B) New York
12. (A) to tell him that his information and prompt reporting of the crime had led to the arrest and conviction of two criminals who the police had been pursuing for much more serious crimes and that he was entitled to a reward of £2,500. (B) telling him that a bag that fitted his description had been found in the house of a recently convicted criminal and that some of the content had also been found. Two weeks later he received a video camera, clothes and jewellery from the police in New York. None of it was, of course, his.

6A A true crime story

Story A

In 1990 Mark Brown went on holiday to Brazil for a month where he spent over £1,000 pounds more than he had planned. His mother had sent him money from England by mail to cover his expenses. He had insured himself before going to Brazil and so he decided on the last day to go to the police and say he had been robbed, and with the report from the police he could claim the money back from the insurance company.

He was so afraid about just happily walking into the police station that he decided that the most convincing way was to fake the robbery in the street. He left all his bags in the hotel and went to a rather dangerous part of São Paulo. After walking up and down the street for half an hour deciding what to do he picked up a telephone and pretended to speak to someone. Suddenly he screamed, 'Help, someone, my bag has been stolen'. To his surprise several people stopped and one man told him to cross the street to where a policeman was standing.

All the people followed him across the road. He was now very nervous and knew he had to continue with his story. He told the policeman that he had left his bag on the floor while making a phone call and that when he looked down it had disappeared. He then began to describe all the things that were in the bag. He had practised this in the afternoon as he knew that the more things he said, the more money he would get. He was so nervous that even though the story wasn't true he started to cry. He gave a description of two men he had seen following him and was told to go to the police station later that day to collect a report for his insurance company.

When he got back to England he sent the police report to the insurance company who told him that every item over £50 required a receipt. He busily spent the next weeks collecting receipts from all the people he knew. He then sent the receipts off to the company and waited. After about five weeks he was sent another letter from the insurance company telling him that he hadn't taken enough care of his bag and that they would not pay any money. Mark couldn't really complain, after all the story was all a fabrication. However, two days later he received a telegram from the police in Brazil to tell him that his information and the prompt reporting of the crime had led to the arrest and conviction of two criminals who the police had been pursuing for much more serious crimes and that he was also entitled to a reward of £2,500.

Story B

In 1990 Mark Brown went on holiday to America for two months where he spent over £1,200 more than he had planned. His mother had sent him money from England by mail to cover his expenses. He had insured himself before going to America and so he decided on the last day to go to the police and say he had been robbed, and with the report from the police he could claim the money back from the insurance company.

He was so afraid about just happily walking into the police station that he decided that the most convincing way was to fake the robbery in the street. He left all his bags in the hotel and went to a rather dangerous part of New York. After walking up and down the street for half an hour deciding what to do, he stood in front of a cigarette machine and bought a pack of cigarettes. Suddenly he screamed, 'Help, someone, my bag has been stolen'. To his surprise several people stopped and one man told him to cross the street to where a policeman was standing.

All the people followed him across the road and he was now very nervous but he knew he had to continue with his story. He told the policeman that he had left his bag on the floor while buying a packet of cigarettes and that when he looked down it had disappeared. He then began to describe all the things that were in the bag. He had practised this in the afternoon as he knew that the more things he said, the more money he would get. He told them he had lost a video camera, jewellery, money and clothes. He wasn't nervous at all. He had always liked acting and totally convinced the police. He gave a description of a man he had seen following him and was told to go to the police station later that day to collect a report for his insurance company.

When he got back to England he sent the police report to the insurance company who told him that every item over £100 required a receipt. He busily spent the next weeks collecting receipts from all the people he knew. He then sent the receipts off to the company and waited. After about five weeks he was sent another letter from the insurance company telling him that he hadn't taken enough care of his bag and that they would not pay any money. Mark couldn't really complain, after all the story was all a fabrication. However, two days later he received a telegram from the police in New York telling him that a bag that fitted his description had been found in the house of a recently convicted criminal and that some of the contents had also been found. Two weeks later he received a video camera, clothes and jewellery from the police in New York. None of it was, of course, his.

TEACHER'S NOTES

6B Making news

Carmen Santos Maldonado

Type of activity
Note writing, news reporting (story telling) and listening. Individual, pair and group work.

Aim
To practise forms of past tense verbs (both regular and irregular).

Task
To put together and tell a story, using picture cards.

Preparation
Make one copy of the worksheet for each group of four or six students. Cut the copies up into cards.

Timing
30–40 minutes

Procedure
1. Divide the class into groups of four or six. Ask the students in each group to sit in a circle and number themselves 1–4 or 1–6, clockwise.
2. Ask the students to imagine that this morning they heard a surprising piece of news on their local radio station and that they are going to tell a friend about it.
3. Give one set of pictures from the worksheet to each group. Ask students number 1 to shuffle the pictures well and deal out four to six pictures face down to every student in the group.
4. Tell the students that they have five to ten minutes to make up a newsworthy story which includes at least three of their pictures. Explain that the story should take one minute to tell. Ask the students to write short notes about the story. Encourage them to be imaginative.
5. Circulate, helping with vocabulary and grammar problems.
6. When the students are ready, tell them that the activity is in two rounds and that they only need half of the stories for the first round.

First round
7. Ask students 1, 3 and 5 to tell their story to the student on their left, beginning with *This morning I heard on the news that ...* Tell the students that the telling-listening periods will be exactly one minute and that you will be giving the 'go' and 'stop' commands.
8. Ask students 2, 4 and 6 to pass the story they have just heard on to the student on their left, again beginning with *This morning I heard on the news that ...*
9. Ask the students to make the stories 'travel' clockwise. Repeat this until the stories have been told to the original storyteller.
10. The original storytellers explain to the whole group what in the story is correct and what has been omitted or changed by showing the pictures they used.

Second round
11. Repeat stages 7–10, with the other half of the stories. Ask students 2, 4 and 6 to start telling their stories.

Follow up
Ask every group to report to the whole class about the most interesting/credible/incredible/imaginative story.

Students can be asked to write a longer version of the story for homework, expanding the initial information.

The conversation can develop into 'stranger-than-fiction stories', real events that the students know about.

Notes & comments
If you don't have even numbers in your class, you can join in, or you can ask your 'odd-number' student to keep the timing for you (after he has made up his own story!).

An element of competition can be introduced by asking the last 'tellers' to guess what pictures the story is based on. Give one point per correctly guessed picture.

6B Making news

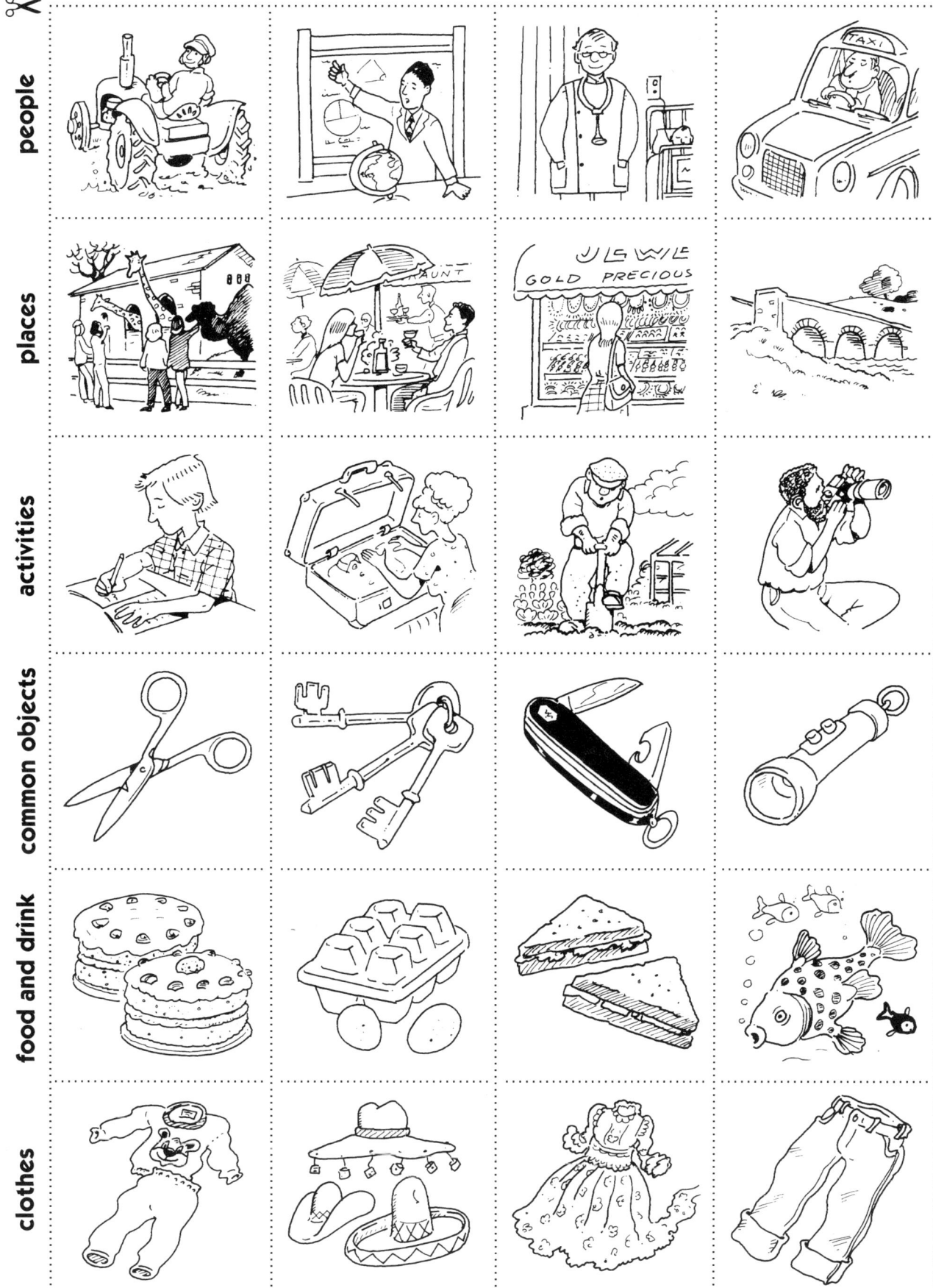

TEACHER'S NOTES

6C Hi! How are you?

Vincent A. Desmond

Type of activity
Mime elicitation (charades).

Aim
To practise using the present perfect for news events.

Task
To mime events.

Preparation
Copy and cut out cue cards – one set for each group.

Timing
20–40 minutes

Procedure
1. Invite a student to ask you 'How are you?' Mime 'Not too good', to show that it's bad news, then mime crashing your car to elicit the 'I've crashed my car' sentence. The first student to come up with the sentence gets the card. After the demonstration explain the rules:
   - The game starts off with one of the team asking, 'How are you?'
   - The person with the card must be silent and explain the sentence with gestures.
   - The first person who says the complete sentence gets the card.
2. Put the students in groups of four or five and give each group a set of cards face down. Students take it in turns to take a card from the top of the pack, to mime and elicit the news.
3. After all the cards have been completed check who has won (the person with most cards in each team wins).

Follow up
Another competition can be played. Someone in the group takes a card and reads the news to the rest of the group. The group members take it in turns to come up with different appropriate responses (*How terrible. I am sorry to hear that*, etc.). The first person to give an inappropriate response or no response at all gets the card, and restarts the game with another card. The person with the fewest cards at the end is the winner.

6C Hi! How are you?

 I've crashed my car.	 My cat has had kittens.	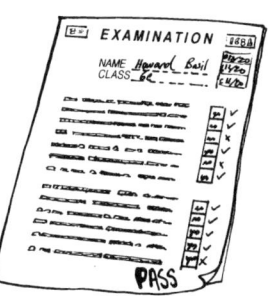 I've passed my exams.	 I've won the lottery.
 I've just had a great holiday.	 I've lost my keys.	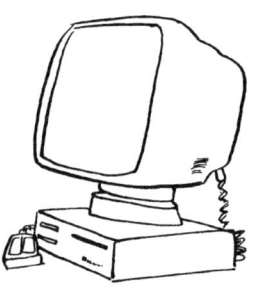 I've just bought a new computer.	 My car's been stolen.
 I've just got a new job.	 I've passed my driving test.	 I haven't done my English homework.	 My brother's been arrested for drink driving.
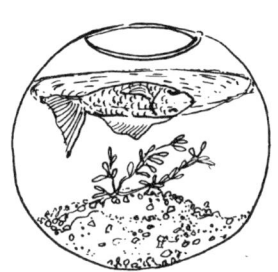 My goldfish has died.	 I've been ill recently.	 I've split up with my fiancé(e).	 I've just met my new boss.

© Sue Kay & Vaughan Jones, 2000. Published by Macmillan Publishers Limited. This sheet may be photocopied and used within the class.

TEACHER'S NOTES

7A *The dinner party*
Nicholas Sheard

Type of activity
Speaking. Pair work and group work.

Aim
To practise expressing opinions and vocabulary of food.

Task
To choose guests for a dinner party, devise a seating plan and write a menu for them.

Preparation
Make one copy of the worksheet for each student.

Timing
45 minutes

Procedure

Part 1

1 Tell the students that they are going to host a dinner party. Explain that this is a dinner party with a difference – they can invite anyone they want, alive or dead.

2 Give one copy of the worksheet to each student and ask them to read through the list of names. Ask them to choose their four guests.

3 After 6 minutes ask the students to stop reading and form pairs. They tell each other which guests they have invited and why. Before this you could pre-teach some of the following language:

- He/she has always been a hero of mine.
- He/she is someone I look up to/admire.
- I would like to talk to him/her about …
- It would be interesting to find out about …
- I love his/her writing/painting/music/work …

4 Explain that each pair is going to draw up a seating plan for their eight guests and themselves. In pairs, students then explain their seating plans to each other.
You could pre-teach this language at this stage:

- They would (probably) have a lot in common …
- They would have a lot to talk about …
- It would be interesting to see how they get on …

Part 2

5 Brainstorm food vocabulary. Tell the students they are going to write a menu for their dinner guests, with a choice of three dishes for each course.

6 Students then compare their menus and vote on the most exotic, original, etc.

Follow up
Give the students name cards of some of the famous people. Then role play the dinner party in large groups or as a class with the students in role, using one or some of the menus that the students have written.

Students research and present or write a short biography of one of the famous people they are particularly interested in.

7A The dinner party

1. You are having a dinner party at home. Who will you want to invite and why? Here are some suggestions.

Wolfgang Amadeus Mozart	Madonna	Mao Tse Tung
Marilyn Monroe	Genghis Khan	Marco Polo
Walt Disney	Christopher Columbus	Moses
Charlie Chaplin	George Washington	Galileo Galilei
Charles Darwin	John Lennon	Catherine the Great
Cleopatra	Karl Marx	Plato
Julius Caesar	Tom Cruise	Albert Einstein
Homer	Mother Teresa	Pablo Picasso
Bill Gates	Princess Diana	Sigmund Freud
William Shakespeare	Michael Jackson	Pablo Neruda
Leonardo da Vinci	Napoleon I	Elvis Presley
Isaac Newton	Alexander the Great	Confucius
Socrates	Nelson Mandela	Pelé

2. Work with a partner. Draw a seating plan for your eight guests and yourselves.

3. Write a menu for your guests. Include at least three dishes for each course.

TEACHER'S NOTES

7B Fiesta

Miguel Ángel Almarza

Type of activity
Reading, speaking and note-taking. Pair and group work.

Aim
To practise presenting information, discussing and decision-making.

Task
To present information to a committee to bid for a contract for the organization of a school trip.
To discuss and decide on the best bid.

Preparation
Make one copy of the worksheet for each group of eight to ten students. Cut up each of the four sections.

Timing
40–50 minutes

Procedure
1. Ask the students in the classroom to form groups of eight, then four pairs within each group.
2. Tell the students that three of the pairs are going to represent tour operators offering school trips to famous festivals. The fourth pair will represent the *Traveljoy Society* appointed by the school to decide on the best bid.
3. Give out a copy of one section of the worksheet to each pair of tour operators and the fourth, the draft form, to the *Traveljoy Society*.
4. Tell the tour operators that they will give a sales presentation based on this information. Allow time for students to read their section, and discuss sales tactics. Will they focus on their tour's cultural interest, linguistic experience, good effects on school life, or on their educational curricula, etc.? Ask them to anticipate how their arguments might be attacked. Ask the members of the committee to read the information available on all three packages in their section and form an initial opinion on what they consider the most interesting trip for the school to subsidize. Circulate, helping with vocabulary and ideas.
5. When the four sub-groups of each big group are ready to start, they should take turns to present their bid. They may follow a model like this: (1) **general information on the festival (where, when, what it is about)**, (2) **accommodation**, (3) **why they think it is good for a school trip**. The committee and the other pairs will make notes to ask questions, ask for more information, etc. When all three pairs have been listened to, the discussion starts until the committee has enough information to come to a decision. They discuss this in private and present their conclusions to all three pairs, giving reasons for their choice.

Follow up
Pairs selling a particular trip get together with other pairs that presented the same trip to compare notes. Alternatively, pairs may write a letter of complaint saying that the decision was fair or unfair, etc.

Notes & comments
It may be a good idea to have a word separately with all the students who are part of the committees of the *Traveljoy Society* while the tour operators are discussing their strategies. At this stage you may suggest how they can elicit information from the tour operators. They should ask them to give reasons for choosing their tour. You could also supervise the preparation work being carried out by the tour operators by suggesting they focus on the best aspects of their trips and how they could minimize the problems that might be brought up by the committee. Let them know that they are allowed to attack the weaknesses of their competitors, so they need to listen to the other presentations attentively.

7B Fiesta

Trip: Second week of July. A five-day stay in the northern Spanish city of Pamplona.

Festival: *San Fermín*: starting on 7th July, *Navarros* celebrate the most widely renowned bullfighting festival, honouring their patron saint. People run with the bulls in the streets every morning. A mixture of fun, tradition and excellent food and wine. An opportunity to meet foreign visitors, attend bullfights and see exciting, colourful street pageants. The countryside surrounding Pamplona is among the most beautiful in Spain. A taste of Spanish culture at its best.

Other interests: Students can edit a magazine with photographs of participants, local newspaper clippings, articles and letters written by students, and also contact international tour operators that organize the same trip to arrange a meeting and form an intercultural club to exchange conversation in English and Spanish.

Trip: A five-day stay visiting Notting Hill Carnival in London. Last week of August.

Festival: *Notting Hill Carnival* takes place on the last weekend of August. Colourful street parades and all-day concerts have been celebrated every year since 1964 in the Notting Hill district, London. Caribbean specialities are served and nearly two million visitors gather together and dance to music in the most famous multiethnic carnival in Europe. Fantastic costumes, great bands, delicious ethnic food.

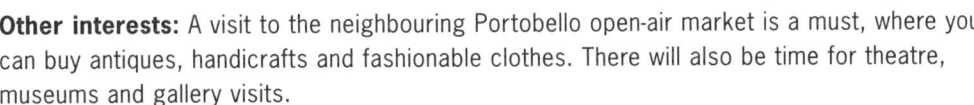

Other interests: A visit to the neighbouring Portobello open-air market is a must, where you can buy antiques, handicrafts and fashionable clothes. There will also be time for theatre, museums and gallery visits.

Trip: Any week between June and September in the Greek capital city of Athens.

Festivals: *The Athens Festival* is held during the summer months and features classical drama at the ancient *Theatre of Herod Atticus* located below the Acropolis. The festival also includes concerts, opera, ballet and modern dance.

Other interests: The trip includes four free tickets per student for theatre performances of classical Greek plays staged in English, plus concerts of their choice, a visit to the Parthenon and Epidaurus theatre and an optional visit to the neighbouring Greek islands.

Your committee has been appointed by the school authorities to listen to three tour operators offering a summer trip for the students of English in your school. Try to get as much information as possible before you decide which is the best bid. Here are the projects in the draft form.

OPERATOR	TRIP	FESTIVAL	DATES	INTEREST
Interfolk Travel	Pamplona, Navarra in the North of Spain	San Fermín, bullfighting festival	Second week of July 5 days	Meet foreign visitors. Traditional Spanish culture. Excellent food and countryside
Honey Tours	London (UK)	Notting Hill Carnival	Last week of August 5 days	Multiethnic event. Good Caribbean and Latin food and music. Guided tours in London
Geoclassics	Athens (Greece)	Athens Festival (arts festival: drama, music and dance)	Summer months One week to choose between June and September	Free tickets for classical performances and concerts. Cultural visits + optional Greek islands trip

> **TEACHER'S NOTES**

8A True or false?
Jon Hird

Type of activity
Reading and writing. Pair work.

Aim
To practise tenses and aspects.

Task
To make a list of true and false statements.

Preparation
Make a copy of the worksheet for each student.

Timing
20–30 minutes

Procedure
1 Give each student a copy of the worksheet.
2 Ask students what the picture means.
3 Tell the class that the man in the picture was doing one of the two activities at noon yesterday. Ask them which they think is the most probable and take a class vote.
4 Ask them to read the rubric. If necessary, demonstrate the activity by giving some sentences about yourself – a mixture of true sentences and lies: *Yesterday I went for a drink with Prince Philip. Then I came home and prepared my lesson.* We recommend you choose something more suitable to the class you are teaching than this sentence. Ask them to decide which are true and which are not.
5 Give a few minutes for students to write out their sentences. Circulate and help with language problems.
6 Ask students to work in pairs, deciding which of their partner's statements are true and which are false. They get a point for each correct guess.

8A True or false?

Complete the following twelve statements about yourself, but write some statements which are *false*. Then exchange papers with a partner. Decide which sentences are true and which are false.

NAME _____

e.g. This morning at 9 o'clock, I was walking to school _____ .

I _____ last week.

Last night at 10 o'clock, I _____ .

I _____ recently.

A few years ago, I _____ .

I _____ this weekend.

At the moment, I _____ .

I think I _____ tonight.

I _____ twice.

I once _____ .

I often _____ .

Next week, I _____ .

I _____ for over ten years.

TEACHER'S NOTES

8B *Dominoes*

Jose Miguel Galarza

Type of activity
Reading. Group work.

Aim
To practise prepositions.

Task
To complete sentences using word dominoes.

Preparation
There are 30 dominoes, so students can play in groups of three, five or six and have the same number each. Make one photocopy of the worksheet for each group. (To make the dominoes last longer, either copy the worksheet directly onto card or stick it down on card and then cut it up.)

Timing
15–20 minutes

Procedure
1 Divide the students into groups of three, five or six.
2 Give one set of dominoes to each group.
3 Explain that they will take it in turns trying to complete the sentences by putting their 'dominoes' down, one at a time. They can add the beginning or ending of a sentence. If they do not have a domino that works, they miss a turn. The first person to have played all their cards wins.
4 Ask students to divide the dominoes so that each person in the group has the same number. The person who has 'back?' on the left card starts.
5 Circulate, checking that students have found the correct connections.

Follow up
Students record the verb + preposition (to sing with, to be good at, etc.).
Students can make their own sets of dominoes using the same or a different language area.

8B Dominoes

back?	Why don't you come	in?	What are you thinking
about?	What did you do that	for?	When are you going
out?	Where do you come	from?	Who are you staring
at?	Who are we waiting	for?	When will they be
back?	What are you talking	about?	What time do you get
up?	What does she live	on?	Who did you give it
to?	Who's she married	to?	What floor do you live
on?	What's the book	about?	What are you listening
to?	What does it depend	on?	What aspect of your job are you best
at?	Who did you have lunch	with?	Why don't you sit
down?	What's the lamb served	with?	Where do you know Jackie
from?	Why don't you take your jacket	off?	Which hotel did you stay
at?	Who's she going out	with?	Who does this belong
to?	Which group did Kurt Cobain sing	with?	What time shall I expect you

TEACHER'S NOTES

8C Phonetics guessing

Ruth Sánchez García

Type of activity
Vocabulary and pronunciation. Group work.

Aim
To practise the recognition of sounds and phonetic symbols.

Task
Vocabulary guessing.

Preparation
Make one copy of the worksheet for each group.

Timing
40–50 minutes

Procedure
1. Divide the students into groups of four to six.
2. Give one copy of the worksheet to each group. Tell students they will also need dice or a coin. Distribute counters if available.
3. Explain that each box has the definition of a word that they must guess. This word contains the sound that appears in brackets.
4. The first player flips a coin. If it is heads, the player moves one square, if it is tails, they move two squares.
   If players guess a word correctly, they stay on that square. If they are wrong, they go back to the previous square.
   When a player lands on a square which has previously been guessed, they must think of another word with the same sound.
5. Circulate, checking that students have given a correct answer.

Key
1. iː TEAM
2. æ CAPITAL
3. ɔː WALL
4. iː PLEASED
5. ɑː FATHER/AUNT
6. ɔː (SURF)BOARD
7. e MESSAGE
8. ɑː PARTNER
9. uː SCHOOL
10. ɪ BUSY
11. ʌ MONTH
12. uː TRUE
13. ɪ LIFT
14. ʌ COME
15. uː HOOLIGANS
16. e FRIEND
17. ʌ UNCLE
18. ʊ WOULD
19. e HEAVY
20. ʌ JUMP
21. ʊ CHILDHOOD
22. e SWEPT
23. ɒ COFFEE
24. ɜː WORDS
25. e HEADLINES
26. ɒ JOB
27. ɜː CHURCH
28. æ MARRY
29. ɔː AUXILIARY
30. ɜː CHURCH

Follow up
Students write the words they have guessed and group them according to the vowel sounds they have in common.

8C Phonetics guessing

TEACHER'S NOTES

9A *By the year 10,000*

Jon Hird

Type of activity
Speaking and writing. Survey/mingle.

Aim
To practise using *will* for predictions.

Task
To produce a class survey of predictions about the future.

Preparation
Make one copy of the worksheet for each student.

Timing
20 minutes

Procedure
1 Divide the class into small groups. For small classes see Notes & comments below.
2 Give each student a copy of the worksheet.
3 Ask the students to tick the 'Yes' and 'No' boxes according to whether or not they agree with the predictions and to add a third prediction of their own to the two already given in each section.
4 Ask the students to ask and answer the questions in their groups, and to record each other's answers.
5 Get the groups to mingle and pool their results. Let the students decide how to organize this.
6 Ask one student to report to the whole class, e.g. *Only six people think that a man will have given birth by the year 2020.* Other students can ask questions if they want to.

Follow up
1 The results could be displayed on a poster/posters entitled 'Our predictions for the future'.
2 Discussion of why people agreed or disagreed with the predictions could be developed.

Notes & comments
Variation: The activity could be a simple pair work exercise, where two students interview each other using all of the predictions. The results are pooled to give the class survey.

9A By the year 10,000

Do you think that by the year 2020 ...   Yes   No

... a man will have given birth?

... we'll all be driving solar-powered cars?

... _____

Do you think that by the year 2050 ...

... humans will have landed on another planet?

... most people will live to be over a hundred?

... _____

Do you think that by the year 2100 ...

... English will be the major world language?

... we'll be having holidays on the moon?

... _____

Do you think that by the year 2500 ...

... we'll be living on nothing but pills?

... the Earth will have been visited by aliens?

... _____

Do you think that by the year 3000 ...

... a person will have lived to be 200?

... there'll only be one religion in the world?

... _____

Do you think that by the year 10,000 ...

... time travel will be possible?

... humans will still exist?

... _____

TEACHER'S NOTES

9B Interpreter

Miguel Ángel Almarza

Type of activity
Role play/Simulation. Group work.

Aim
To practise reported speech.

Task
To simulate an act of communication between two people that speak different languages with the help of an interpreter.

Preparation
Make one copy of the worksheet for each group. Cut up the role cards and hand them out to the groups in a pile face down.

Timing
30 minutes

Procedure
1 Introduce the activity by telling or asking the students what it feels like to be in a foreign country where you don't speak the language. Elicit some of the most embarrassing or difficult situations for the traveller.
2 Ask students to form groups of three. In each group there are three roles:
   - police officer
   - foreigner
   - interpreter

   If there are four students in a group, double up the role of foreigner.
3 Explain that in each group the foreigner(s) takes a role card at random from the pile. The card describes a situation. They will have to explain it to the police officer, who does not speak English, via the interpreter.
4 If necessary, demonstrate one of the situations with two students.
5 Make sure that they take turns to change roles for the subsequent cards so that everyone gets the chance to be the police officer, the foreigner and the interpreter.

Follow up
Allow some time at the end of the group work to role play some of the situations in front of the whole class – those that have worked best with the smaller groups. (Make notes as you monitor group work on particularly productive and generative situations and groups for a final demonstration.)

Notes & comments
It is important to let the students know that when they act as police officers they do not understand a word of English (they need the interpreter). When they act as foreigners English is the only language they are allowed to use. It is only when they act as interpreters that they are bilingual. This activity may work better with a monolingual class.

9B Interpreter

You look like a famous soap star in the country that you are visiting. Fans keep taking you for this celebrity. You want a quiet holiday and are fed up with people stopping you in the street. You want to know who you look like so much. Discuss the possibility of police protection.	**Y**ou've been reported to the police for having started a fight in a restaurant. In fact you were attacked by one of the waiters because you were complaining about the bad service.
You've been caught shoplifting. This is really embarrassing for you. You had never done anything like this before. You are willing to pay a fine if this is the law. You don't want a scandal. You are a politician in your country.	**Y**ou saw a young man dropping a suspicious-looking bag into a litter bin in a touristy area. You followed him to his car, where you saw him hide a gun.
You are a futurologist and want to warn the authorities of some approaching natural disaster. You can feel in your body that an earthquake or hurricane winds will cause trouble. The place must be evacuated in 24 hours.	**Y**ou've been overcharged by a taxi driver on the way from the airport to your hotel. You were not familiar with the notes and paid the money that he asked for. You now realize that it was definitely too much.
You've missed a travelling companion at the airport. You think he or she has been kidnapped. You'll have to give full details and ask for help.	**W**hen you went to get your expensive camera back from the hotel safe it had gone. The hotel manager says he is not responsible for stolen valuables left in the hotel unless you show him your receipt. You've lost it.
You've lost your credit card and traveller's cheques and have only a little cash left. Everybody you know that could help you out from your country is on holiday. Your bank does not answer your phone calls.	**Y**ou've had a car crash in a rented vehicle. The car-hire company says you have to pay for your hospital expenses and damages to the car. You are sure you signed for fully comprehensive insurance when you hired the car.

TEACHER'S NOTES

9C *The wedding*
Nicholas Sheard

Type of activity
Pronunciation. Individual study and pair work.

Aim
To practise the sound /ə/ in connected speech.

Task
To read out a dialogue, focusing on the sound /ə/.

Preparation
Make one copy of the worksheet for each student.

Timing
40 minutes

Procedure
1 Ask the students to imagine that they are getting married. Using the pictures, brainstorm the different things that need to be arranged before the wedding day.
2 Write these words on the board: *vicar, best man, groom, caterers, call off, see to (something), go out with, carnations, buttonholes*. Check that the meaning is clear, using the pictures, and drill for pronunciation.
3 Tell the students that they are going to read a conversation between a bride and groom who are finalizing plans for their wedding. Give one copy of the worksheet to each student.
4 Ask the students to form pairs. Explain that they are going to read the dialogue, focusing in particular on the sound /ə/, which is marked in the text on the worksheet. Model and drill example sentences from the dialogue in open class to illustrate this.
5 Circulate and monitor the pairs, helping them with pronunciation.
6 Ask a few of the pairs to perform their dialogue for the whole class, using props if they are available. Strong students might like to try to perform the dialogue (or an approximation of it) without looking at the worksheet.

Follow up
The students could extend the dialogue for homework, performing their version in the next lesson.

9C The wedding

B = Bride; G = Groom

B: Roses ə carnatəns?

G: Sorry, what wəs that?

B: Roses ə carnatəns? Fər thə buttənholes.

G: Də we need flowəs?

B: Wəll, yes. I'd like thəm.

G: Flowəs ə very expensive, yə know Vəronicə. We've already spent too much.

B: Bət it *is* ə specəl day, John.

G: OK. How əbout red roses?

B: Red? No! Lində Evəns had red roses at *her* wedding.

G: So?

B: Well, didn't yə use tə go out with hər?

G: Yes, so what?

B: Well I don't want *our* wedding tə be like *hers*.

G: Yə're not still jealəs əf hər, are you?

B: Jealəs? Me? Jealəs? əf course I'm not. Yə *did* go out with hə fə four years, though.

(There is an uncomfortable silence)

B: Həve yə booked thə honeymoon yet?

G: No, I havən't booked thə honeymoon. I've been too busy.

B: What about thə catərərs? Həve yə spokən tə thəm əbout thə menu?

G: No, I havən't.

B: ənd thə man who'll be doing thə disco?

G: No.

B: Thə vicər əbout thə church service?

G: No.

B: Thə phətogrəphə?

G: No.

B: The flowəs fə thə church?

G: I thought *you* wə going tə see tə thəm.

B: I can't bəlieve this. Wə not evən married yet, ənd wə're arguing already!

(There is a pause)

G: Look Vəronicə, maybe we shəd wait ə while.

B: What?

G: Before we get married.

B: What ə yə saying, John?

G: I'm saying thət I think we shəd call off thə wedding.

TEACHER'S NOTES

10A How well organized are you?

Carmen Santos Maldonado

Type of activity

Speaking, listening and note-taking. Individual and pair work.

Aim

To practise lexis relating to time and personal organization.

Task

To complete a questionnaire about personal organization and time management.

Preparation

Make one copy of the worksheet for every pair of students. Cut copies into A and B.

Timing

About 20 minutes

Procedure

1. Tell the students that they are going to interview each other about their personal organization and time management.
2. Divide the students into pairs and assign A and B within each pair.
3. Give A and B students their part of the questionnaire.
4. Ask the students to read the instructions and answer their questionnaires, noting their own answers on the side.
5. Circulate and help with vocabulary problems.
6. Tell the students to start interviewing each other and to make a note of their partner's answers.
7. Write the scoring system on the board.
8. Ask the students to calculate their score in their own questionnaire and that of their partner, to see who's better organized.

Follow up

A conversation could be developed about useful tips for time-saving and better self-organization, either in the pairs or as a whole class.

Notes & comments

Encourage the students to ask follow up questions, to make the interview more natural.
Encourage students to ask the questions, rather than let the partner 'read' them, so that everybody makes an effort for oral communication.
Suggest that they take it in turns to ask one question each. This makes it more entertaining, and gives everybody roughly the same opportunity to speak (if time is limited).

Scoring system

QUESTIONNAIRE A

1 a 3	b 2	c 1
2 a 2	b 1	c 3
3 a 2	b 1	
4 a 1	b 3	c 2
5 a 1	b 2	
6 a 2	b 1	c 3
7 a 2	b 1	

QUESTIONNAIRE B

1 a 1	b 2	
2 a 1	b 3	c 2
3 a 3	b 2	c 1
4 a 1	b 2	c 3
5 a 1	b 2	
6 a 1	b 2	
7 a 3	b 2	c 1

TOTAL SCORE

Up to 15 points: You are a disaster. You can't get things done on time because of a total lack of organization. You should make a plan to start organizing your life today!

Between 16–28 points: You are fairly well organized. On the whole you get things done when they need to be done. You must, however, be aware of a certain tendency to improvise, which may cause you some problems.

Between 29–36 points: You are very well organized. You manage your time extremely well and don't like leaving things to chance. However, keep in mind that your liking for organization could verge on obsession.

INSIDE OUT *Resource Pack*

10A *How well organized are you?*

A

Here are some questions about how well you organize your time. Answer them yourself, then ask your partner, making a note of both answers.

	YOU	YOUR PARTNER

1. How do you normally keep your desk?   **a)** Perfectly tidy.   **b)** Once a week I have to tidy it up before things get too untidy.   **c)** It's a mess.

2. How punctual are you for your appointments, classes, work, etc.?
   a) Very early.   **b)** Late.   **c)** On time.

3. When it comes to organization, what reputation do you have among your friends and family? They think I'm …   **a)** a well-organized person.   **b)** a bit of a disaster.

4. Do you have a diary where you write what you have to do during the day/week/month?   **a)** No.   **b)** Yes, I use it all the time.   **c)** Yes, but I hardly use it.

5. Do you find time to relax every day?   **a)** Not really, I always seem to have things to do.   **b)** Yes, I usually keep some time free during the day to relax.

6. When you have a piece of work to do for your work or studies, how do you organize yourself?   **a)** I work to the last minute to finish it.   **b)** I start the day before the deadline.   **c)** I finish a week in advance.

7. For your friends' and family's birthdays and anniversaries, do you get round to writing or phoning in good time?   **a)** Yes, I normally do.   **b)** No, I'm usually too late.

✂ ....

B

Here are some questions about how well you organize your time. Answer them yourself, then ask your partner, making a note of both answers.

	YOU	YOUR PARTNER

1. Do you find that you frequently run out of essentials, like sugar or toilet paper?
   a) Yes, I only remember to buy a new supply when I've run out.   **b)** No, I usually buy a new supply before I run out.

2. Do you normally write a list of 'things to do'?   **a)** No, I hate planning.   **b)** Yes, and I try to stick to it.   **c)** Yes, but I never manage to do all the things on the list.

3. When you have to do something or go somewhere, do you often …
   a) get up early?   **b)** get up on time but end up rushing?   **c)** get up late?

4. When you get home from a trip, what do you do with your luggage?   **a)** I don't unpack for days.   **b)** I start unpacking almost immediately but leave things in the way.
   c) A couple of hours after getting home everything is back in its place.

5. Have you ever missed a train/plane/coach because you didn't give yourself enough time?   **a)** Yes.   **b)** No, I always allow plenty of time.

6. Do you often leave the dishes unwashed or the bed unmade for more than one day?
   a) Very often.   **b)** Almost never.

7. How do you normally keep your wardrobe?   **a)** Always perfectly tidy.   **b)** Once a week I have to tidy it before clothes start piling up.   **c)** It's a mess.

© Sue Kay & Vaughan Jones, 2000. Published by Macmillan Publishers Limited. This sheet may be photocopied and used within the class.   **Photocopiable**

TEACHER'S NOTES

10B Rules and regulations

Miguel Ángel Almarza

Type of activity
Collaborative writing.

Aim
To practise using modals of obligation and permission.
To practise paraphrasing.

Task
To write a set of rules and regulations (obligation, permission, prohibition and no obligation) that apply to a given place.

Preparation
Make one copy of the worksheet and cut it up into cards.

Timing
30–40 minutes

Procedure
1. Divide the students into small groups.
2. Give a card to each group.
3. Tell the students that the aim of the task is to produce a poster giving eight rules for the place on the card. They must strictly follow the instructions about forbidden words: see the lists headed 'Don't use these' on the worksheet.
4. Write the modals below on the board:

   You have to/must
   You mustn't
   You can
   You cannot
   You don't have to/needn't

5. Number the posters and display them around the classroom. Ask the students to read all the posters and guess the place that each applies to.

INSIDE OUT *Resource Pack*

10B *Rules and regulations*

Write a set of rules and regulations for one of these places.
There are some *taboo* words that you are <u>not allowed to use</u>.

○ LIBRARY

Don't use these
borrow
books
smoke
eat
magazines

○ ZOO

Don't use these
animals
food
cage
security area
grass

○ CINEMA

Don't use these
sit
pop corn
film
refreshments
talk

○ PUB

Don't use these
drink
pay
dance
consumption
tables

○ AMUSEMENT PARK

Don't use these
ride
attraction
ticket
queue
lawn

○ FOOTBALL STADIUM

Don't use these
referee
football players
pitch
shout
cheer

○ HOSPITAL

Don't use these
smoke
patients
disturb
corridor
quiet

○ AIRPORT

Don't use these
trolley
baggage
check-in
gifts
boarding pass

© Sue Kay & Vaughan Jones, 2000. Published by Macmillan Publishers Limited. This sheet may be photocopied and used within the class.

Photocopiable

TEACHER'S NOTES

10C Detectives

Vincent A. Desmond

Type of activity
Deduction and speculation game. Group work.

Aim
To practise time expressions/discussion.

Task
To piece together a story using clues.

Preparation
Make one copy of the worksheet per group of three or four students and cut it up as indicated.

Timing
20–30 minutes

Procedure

1. Introduce the situation and the characters to the class and explain they will try and find out what happened and why.
   - Tony, the victim, was found dead today. He had been shot with his own gun.
   - Jeanette was Tony's wife.
   - Steve was Tony and Jeanette's driver.
   - Peter was Tony's business partner.

2. Divide the class into groups of three or four.

3. Hand out the clues from the worksheet – one set to each group. Give each student a different set of clues, so that each has all the information about one of the four characters.

4. Tell the students to exchange the clues they have and come up with a theory explaining Tony's murder.

5. When they have finished, groups report back to the class with their theories on who did what and why.

Answer
You can either choose the explanation which is the most ingenious or entertaining – or decide which group got closer to the version below.

Steve and Peter both needed money. Steve's salary was small. Peter had lost a fortune gambling. They had been stealing from the business together for a year. To divert suspicion they pretended to hate each other. But the money still wasn't enough – especially for Peter.

Peter played tennis with Jeanette and he knew she had fallen in love with him. He persuaded her to leave her husband and run away to Bangkok with him, though he had no intention of actually going. She bought the tickets and cleared out her and Tony's joint private bank account. There was about £2,000,000 in it: the savings from Tony's share of profits of the business. Meanwhile Peter booked a flight to Rio.

Tony had long before realized money was disappearing from the business and he had hired a private detective. The detective told Tony about Jeanette's visit to the bank and when Tony discovered that she had emptied the account, he confronted her. She panicked and shot him.

Follow up
Students write up a report or a newspaper story telling what happened.

10C Detectives

Tony has been found dead today at home. He had been shot with his own gun. The police have the following information about him.

- [ ] He hired a private detective a month ago.
- [ ] The business he owns with Peter has been in trouble for over a year.
- [ ] His marriage was not a happy one.

Tony has been found dead today at home. He had been shot with his own gun. Steve was the driver for Tony and Peter's business. The police have the following information about him.

- [ ] He's always arguing with Peter at work and last week they had a fight.
- [ ] He owes three months' rent on his flat.
- [ ] He has a criminal conviction for theft.

Tony has been found dead today at home. He had been shot with his own gun. Jeanette was Tony's wife. The police have the following information about her.

- [ ] She plays tennis regularly with Peter.
- [ ] She has a plane ticket for Bangkok for the day after tomorrow.
- [ ] She wasn't happy in her marriage.
- [ ] She went to her bank the day before yesterday and took out all the money from the joint account she held with Tony: about £2,000,000.

Tony has been found dead today at home. He had been shot with his own gun. Peter was Tony's business partner. The police have the following information about him.

- [ ] He has plane tickets for Rio tomorrow and Bangkok the day after – both from London.
- [ ] He is a regular gambler.
- [ ] He's just sold his flat and is staying in a hotel.
- [ ] He's always arguing with Steve at work and last week they had a fight.
- [ ] He plays tennis regularly with Jeanette.
- [ ] Tony and Peter's business has been in trouble for over a year.

TEACHER'S NOTES

11A Useless information
Russell Stannard

Type of activity
Speaking, listening. Mill drill.

Aim
To practise numbers.

Task
To exchange information.

Preparation
Make one copy of the worksheet for each student and cut it in two.
Cut out enough of the facts for each student to have at least one.

Timing
20 minutes

Procedure
1. Give out one copy of the numbers grid to each student.
2. Give each student one 'fact'. If there are fewer than 16 students, give them two or three facts each.
3. Tell the students to write the fact beside the corresponding number on the numbers grid. At this stage you should check for any individual problems with vocabulary.
4. Tell the students that they have to move around the class and gather as many other facts as possible.
   - Explain that they can only pass on two facts to any given student and receive two facts.
   - Explain that they can pass on facts that were given to them by other students.
   - Explain that the facts should be noted down by their corresponding numbers.
5. While students are doing the activity write the numbers up on the board.
6. When students have finished get individual students to come up to the board and fill in the correct information by the number.

Follow up
Put the students into pairs. Tell them they have (five) minutes to memorize the facts, then ask one student in each pair to turn over the sheet. The other one tests him or her to see how many they can remember.

A 'Ten million'   B 'Ten million is the average number of times you blink in one year.'

Get them to test each other out of 10 and then see who remembered the most facts in the class.

Notes & comments
An alternative procedure is to put the students into groups of three and make one person in the group the writer. Cut up the facts and give each group a set. The other two students look at the facts one by one and dictate the information to the writer who completes the numbers grid.
A second alternative is to put the students into groups of three. One student is the writer and the other two are runners. Stick the facts on the walls around the class. The runners in each group read the facts and then go back to the writer and dictate the facts to him or her. The winner is the first group to finish and have all the information correctly written down.

11A Useless information

Numbers

Number	Details
20 seconds	
10,000,000	
18 acres	
1.5 kilos	
20 minutes	
80 km/h	
2 years	
2,000,000	
2 (twice)	
150 calories	
1140	
9 years	
3,200 kilos	
150 times	
300 bones	
4,000 gallons	

Facts

The Apollo 11 only had 20 seconds of fuel left when it landed.	You blink over 10,000,000 times a year.	The American population, on average, eats 18 acres of pizza a day.	Your brain weighs about 1.5 kilos.
A fully loaded super tanker takes 20 minutes to stop.	A car travelling at 80 km/h uses half its fuel to overcome wind resistance.	The average person spends about 2 years on the phone in a lifetime.	The odds of being killed by lightning are 1 in 2,000,000.
Termites eat wood twice as fast when they listen to rock music.	Banging your head against the wall burns 150 calories in one hour.	The average person makes 1140 phone calls each year.	Right-handed people live on average 9 years longer than left-handed people.
When the Titanic sank there were about 3,200 kilos of ham on board.	The average flea can jump 150 times its body length.	You are born with 300 bones but as an adult you have 206.	A jumbo uses 4,000 gallons of petrol to take off.

> TEACHER'S NOTES

11B Postcards

Vincent A. Desmond

Type of activity
Writing – gap-filling. Pair work.

Aim
To enable learners to practise the language of describing places, travel and geographical location.

Task
To complete two postcards – one sent from a bad holiday, one from a good holiday.

Preparation
Make one copy of the worksheet for each pair of students.

Timing
20 minutes

Procedure
1 Divide the students into pairs.
2 Hand out the worksheets – one per pair of students – with a good postcard and a bad postcard to fill in.
3 Ask the students to complete the two postcards describing a good holiday and a bad holiday. Tell them that they can use one or more words to fill each space.
4 When the students have finished their postcards they read each other's to decide who had the best holiday and who had the worst holiday.

Notes & comments
There is enormous variation in how the postcard can be completed. Students may need help using the adverbs correctly (*absolutely*, *quite*, etc.) as well as with vocabulary. Note *look forward to ____ ing.*

11B Postcards

Dear _____ ,

Hi! I'm having a really __*wonderful*__ time here in _____ .
The weather's so _____ which is _____ for me.
I'm staying in a _____ which is really _____ .

The people here are absolutely _____ and they always
_____ . I have met someone called _____ who is
very _____ – we _____ every day.

There is _____ to do here. Yesterday I went _____ ,
which I thought was _____ , and tomorrow I'm going
_____ which should be _____ .

The food is really _____ and I drank some local
_____ which tasted _____ . Anyway, I'm
looking forward to _____ .
Love,
_____

Dear _____ ,

Hi! I'm having a really __*terrible*__ time here in _____ .
The weather's so _____ which is _____ for me. I'm staying
in a _____ which is really _____ .

The people here are absolutely _____ and they always
_____ . I have met someone called _____ who is
very _____ – we _____ every day.

There is _____ to do here. Yesterday I went _____ ,
which I thought was _____ , and tomorrow I'm going
_____ which should be _____ .

The food is really _____ and I drank some local
_____ which tasted _____ . Anyway, I'm
looking forward to _____ .
Love,
_____

TEACHER'S NOTES

11C *Globetrotters*

Tania Bastow and Ceri Jones

Type of activity
Pair work and group discussion.

Aim
To practise the present perfect.

Task
To choose the best candidate for an award.

Preparation
Make one photocopy of the worksheet for each student.

Timing
30 minutes

Procedure
1. Divide the class into groups.
2. Tell the students that they have to award the 'Globetrotter Extraordinaire' trophy. Give each student a copy of the worksheet.
3. Allow a couple of minutes for silent reading. Circulate, checking that students have understood.
4. Ask the students, to discuss the questions and complete each line with the name of one student in the group.
5. After the discussion the students decide who to award the trophy to.
6. Let the spokesman/woman for each group announce the winners.

Follow up
Ask the students to write a prize-giving speech for the award ceremony.

11C Globetrotters

Who in your group ...

has used the greatest number of different forms of transport?	(100 points)	_____
has used the most unusual form of transport?	(100 points)	_____
has visited the most continents?	(100 points)	_____
has visited the most capital cities?	(100 points)	_____
can say 'Thank you' in the most languages?	(100 points)	_____
can count to ten in the most languages?	(100 points)	_____
has spent the least time in his/her own country in the last twelve months?	(100 points)	_____
has been on the longest journey?		
(a) number of hours from start to finish	(100 points)	_____
(b) number of kilometres from start to finish	(100 points)	_____
has spent the most time in a foreign country?	(100 points)	_____
has eaten the most unusual food?	(100 points)	_____

Our

Globetrotter Extraordinaire

is _____

TEACHER'S NOTES

12A *Lies and statistics*
Russell Stannard

Type of activity
Speaking and reading. Team game.

Aim
To practise speaking and listening.

Task
To determine which facts are true, and which are false. Sentence auction.

Preparation
Make a copy of the worksheet for each group. Cut the worksheets in two as indicated.

Timing
30 minutes

Procedure
1. Divide the class into groups of four or five.
2. Give each group a copy of the top half of the worksheet but not the answers.
3. Explain that some of the sentences are true, some false. Allow a few minutes for silent reading.
4. Use the picture on the worksheet to introduce the concept of an auction. Elicit/check vocabulary such as *bid*, *bidder*, etc. and ask concept questions like: 'Are prices fixed beforehand at an auction?'.
5. Explain the rules of the game.
   - The teacher is the auctioneer.
   - Each group has £2,000 which they must use to buy as many <u>true</u> sentences as they can.
   - Groups get one point for each true sentence they buy.
   - Money is deducted from their total whether the sentence is true or false.
   - The winning group is the one with the most points when all the sentences have been auctioned.
6. Give the groups a few minutes to decide together which sentences they want to buy, and how much they will pay for them.
7. Auction the sentences one at a time. As each sentence is sold, tell the group whether they have bought a true or false sentence.
   If no one wants to buy a sentence and you are unable to trick or convince the students that it is true, move on to the next sentence, having told the class the real fact.

Follow up
An alternative is to cut the worksheet up and distribute the sentences. Students move around the class collecting all the facts. Once they have done this they sit down and decide if they think the facts are true or false. The class then has a vote to decide whether the fact is true or false. If the students guessed correctly it is a point for the students. If the students guessed incorrectly it is a point for the teacher.
Another way to play the game is to put the students in groups of four or five and simply photocopy all the pieces of information, cut them up and put them in a pile in the middle of the group. The students turn them over, read what the information is about and decide together whether it is true or false. Remember this will not produce a lot of discussion but students will be interested in the phrases and so a lot of reading and comprehension work will be achieved.

Notes & comments
If you have access to an OHP, you can run the auction without giving the students a chance to see the sentences first. Or, you can write them on the board.
See student's Book, page 45 where there is a similar activity.

12A *Lies and statistics*

1. The most common name in the world is John.
2. The Queen of England has two birthdays.
3. Your nose never stops growing.
4. When you eat celery you burn more calories chewing it than you take in.
5. A mile in the sea and a mile on land are not the same.
6. The longest frontier is between China and Russia.
7. You cannot keep your eyes open when you sneeze.
8. The biggest pizza was made in America.
9. Alaska used to be part of Russia.
10. The biggest pyramid is in Mexico.
11. The Spanish drink the most coffee per person in the world.
12. The Americans eat more meat than any other nation.
13. George I, King of England, could not speak English.
14. The biggest-selling album in the world is *Thriller* by Michael Jackson.
15. Blondes have more hair than dark-haired people.
16. Elvis Presley is the biggest-selling artist in the world of music.
17. Your eyes are the same size all your life, they never grow.
18. Women blink more than men.

Answers

1. False. The most common name in the world is Mohammed.
2. True. The Queen has an official birthday and her real one.
3. True. Your nose grows throughout your life and so do your ears.
4. True.
5. True. A nautical mile is longer; it is 6,080 feet and a land mile is 5,280 feet.
6. False. The longest frontier is between Canada and the United States; it is 6,416 km long.
7. True. Actually when you sneeze all your bodily functions stop for a second, including your heart. This means that your eyes close.
8. False. The biggest pizza was made in South Africa.
9. True. They sold it to America for about 2 cents per acre. Alaska is a vast area with incredible natural resources.
10. True. It is about sixty miles from Mexico City and it covers more than 40 acres. The great pyramid at Giza covers 13 acres.
11. False. Surprisingly it is the Swedish who drink the most coffee per person in the world.
12. False. The Argentinians eat the most meat.
13. True. And he had no intention of learning. He ruled between 1714 and 1727.
14. True.
15. True. In fact it is nearly double the amount.
16. True.
17. True.
18. True. In fact they blink nearly twice as frequently.

© Sue Kay & Vaughan Jones, 2000. Published by Macmillan Publishers Limited. This sheet may be photocopied and used within the class.

Teacher's Notes

12B *Food, sleep and shelter*

Nicholas Sheard

Type of activity
Vocabulary. Group work.

Aim
To revise and reinforce vocabulary from Unit 12 in Inside Out Student's Book.

Task
To put words in the correct category.

Preparation
Make one photocopy of the worksheet for each group and cut it up as indicated.

Timing
15 minutes

Procedure
1 Divide the students into groups of three. Give each group a set of cards.
2 Write *Food*, *Sleep* and *Shelter* at the top of the board. Ask the students to find one or two examples of words in each category.
3 Explain that they have twenty vocabulary cards for each of the three categories. In their groups they have to sort the words into the three categories. The winner is the first group to categorize all their words successfully. Monitor the activity, helping with any vocabulary problems that arise.
4 Ask the students to shuffle all the cards together and put the stack face down on the table.
Ask the students to turn over the top card. Explain that in turn they will each turn over the top card. If three on the run are from the same category, then the first student to shout 'SNAP' wins the round and picks up all the cards that have been turned over.

The activity then continues with the winner of the previous round turning over the next card. The winner is the student with the most cards when the teacher ends the activity.

FOOD
oyster	olive oil	house red	vitamins	dessert
fig	spinach	curry	tasty	bland
grilled	garlic	oily	organic	deep fried
greasy	crunchy	tender	spicy	burnt

SLEEP
dream	snore	yawn	sleepwalk	lie-in
insomnia	nightmare	night owl	nap	sleepy
early bird	alarm clock	lullaby	duvet	tired
teddy bear	wake up	get up	double bed	pyjamas

SHELTER
caravan	hostel	flat	narrow-boat	igloo
tent	shed	tree house	apartment	hotel
greenhouse	hut	bungalow	bed & breakfast	house
garage	shack	marquee	conservatory	wigwam

12B Food, sleep and shelter

Put these words into the correct groups. There are twenty words in each group.

alarm clock	apartment	bed & breakfast	bland	bungalow
burnt	caravan	conservatory	crunchy	curry
deep fried	dessert	double bed	dream	duvet
early bird	fig	flat	garage	garlic
get up	greasy	greenhouse	grilled	hostel
hotel	house	house red	hut	igloo
insomnia	lie-in	lullaby	marquee	nap
narrow-boat	nightmare	night owl	oily	olive oil
organic	oyster	pyjamas	shack	shed
sleepwalk	sleepy	snore	spicy	spinach
tasty	teddy bear	tender	tent	tired
tree house	vitamins	wake up	wigwam	yawn

TEACHER'S NOTES

12C Just a minute!
Ruth Sánchez García

Type of activity
Filling in a table. Whole class or group work.

Aim
To practise countable and uncountable nouns.

Task
To fill in a grid with countable and uncountable nouns.

Preparation
Make one copy of the worksheet for each student.

Timing
20–30 minutes

Procedure
1. Give one copy of the worksheet to each student.
2. Ask the students to look carefully at the grid on the worksheet. Point out to them that there are six columns with quantifiers as headings.
3. Explain the rules of the game to the students:
   - Students have to complete the lines with words that fit the categories you are going to read aloud. If necessary, remind the students of the rules for quantifiers and countable/uncountable nouns.
   - Students have a maximum of one minute to come up with a word under each heading and they must write only one word per category.
   - If a student completes their entire line before the time is up, they have to say *Stop!* and the rest of the class must stop writing.
   - Students score one point for every correct word and two points for every 'original' word – a word that only one student has written.
   - The winner of the game is the student with the most points.
4. Read out the first category from the list below. If nobody finishes after one minute, call *Stop!*.

List of categories
1. Something you have in the kitchen.
2. Something you can't live without.
3. Something you had when you were a child.
4. Something you would like to have.
5. Something you can put in your pocket.
6. Something you are wearing now.
7. Something in the classroom.
8. Something you can see in the street.
9. Something you can buy with your pocket money/salary.
10. Something you would like for your next birthday.

5. The students say their words. Check that the words are grammatically correct and are appropriate for the context.
6. Give the students their points and carry on with the second category on the list.

Follow up
Once you have finished your categories, encourage the students to add some more.
If the students have enjoyed the game, you can use the same procedure to practise any other grammar or lexical field (e.g. vocabulary categories: clothes, food, sports, etc.).

12C *Just a minute!*

	1	2	3	4	5	6	7	8	9	10
only one										
a couple of										
lots of										
several										
a little										
a few										

TEACHER'S NOTES

13A Know-it-alls

Vincent A. Desmond

Type of activity
Reading, writing, listening and speaking.
Mill drill.

Aim
To practise asking and answering questions.

Task
To prepare and ask questions about other students' areas of knowledge.

Preparation
Make one copy of the worksheet for each student and cut the copies in two. Provide yourself with something to fix cards to the classroom wall with.

Timing
20 minutes

Procedure
1 Hand out Know-it-all cards, one per student. Students write their names and two things they know something about. This could range from computers to football, and from music to the history of the local area.
2 Put the cards up around the classroom.
3 Hand out the question forms. Students look at all the cards and write three questions for two people whose area they are interested in. These could range from personal questions ('How long have you …?') to factual questions ('What is a CD-ROM?').
4 Students then go and ask their questions.
5 Students share anything interesting they have found out about each other.

13A *Know-it-alls*

My specialist subjects are …

Name: _____

Subject 1: _____

Subject 2: _____

✂ ···

I'd like to know …

1

Name: _____

Question 1: _____

Question 2: _____

Question 3: _____

2

Name: _____

Question 1: _____

Question 2: _____

Question 3: _____

TEACHER'S NOTES

13B *Make & do*
Jon Hird

Type of activity
Mime game/drill.

Aim
To revise and practise collocations of *make* and *do*.

Task
To mime an action involving a *make* or *do* expression for other students to guess.

Preparation
Make one copy of the worksheet and cut it up as indicated.

Timing
15–20 minutes

Procedure
1 If possible, ask the students to sit in a circle or horseshoe.
2 Give one card to each student.
3 Tell the students that they are going to mime the expression on their card. Give a couple of examples, e.g. *do the ironing* or *make a sandwich* and get the students to guess them.
4 Give the students a few seconds to think of a way of miming the expression. Help them if necessary.
5 The first student mimes their expression. When another student guesses what it is, they shout it out. When the expression is correctly guessed, the next student in the circle starts miming.
6 The process continues round the circle, with each student miming *all* the expressions that came before, while the other students simultaneously chorus the expression. So for example, student number ten will have to mime the previous nine as well as their own.
7 The activity continues until all the students have mimed the expressions on their cards.

Notes & comments
This activity works with anything up to twenty students. For larger classes, divide the students into two groups and have two independent activities going on.
Before the activity, the cards can be used to check or teach the collocations. (1) Put the students into small groups and give each group a set of cards. Get the students to group the cards according to whether they are *make* or *do* expressions. (2) Give each student a card and get the students to stand in two groups according to whether they have a *make* or *do* expression.

13B Make & do

a decision	a mistake	money	the bed
a mess	a phone call	dinner	a noise
an effort	friends	an appointment	a coffee
up your mind	a sandwich	your best	some work
the cleaning	the driving	some damage	nothing
the ironing	the shopping	the cooking	someone a favour
your homework	yoga	the washing	the washing up

TEACHER'S NOTES

13C Feng Shui

Tania Bastow and Ceri Jones

Type of activity
Speaking. Group work.

Aim
To review and practise various structures, including conditionals.

Task
To follow instructions to furnish an office according to the rules of Feng Shui.

Preparation
Make one copy of the worksheet for each group of three students.

Timing
30 minutes

Procedure
1. Ask the students if they know anything about Feng Shui.

   Feng Shui (pronounced 'Feng Shway' (Mandarin), 'Fung Shui' (Cantonese) or 'Fung Shuway' (American)) means wind and water. It is an ancient Chinese study of the natural and 'built' environment. It analyses how a building and environment interact with the occupants and gives recommendations how to improve this relationship.

2. Tell the students that they are Feng Shui consultants and that they have been called in by a small company to help them boost their profits and productivity.
3. Divide the students into groups of three.
4. Give each group a copy of the worksheet. Allow a couple of minutes for them to read the instructions.
5. Ask the students to decide how to furnish the office and how to draw up a plan. Refer them to 'The Top Ten Tips'.
6. Circulate, helping with vocabulary and other problems.
7. When all the students have finished, display the plans on the walls of the classroom and ask the groups to circulate, evaluating and criticizing each design according to the Feng Shui rules.
8. When all the groups have had a chance to evaluate all the plans ask each group to vote for the best solution. (They cannot vote for their own design.)

Follow up
Feng Shui your classroom. In groups, draw a floor plan. Include windows, doors, staircases, etc. Decide which direction (north, east, south or west) the entrance faces.
Now use 'The Top Ten Tips' to redesign your classroom.

13C Feng Shui

You are a Feng Shui consultant. You have been called in to help a small company boost their profits and productivity. Here is a floor plan of their office. You have been asked to furnish it so that it can be shared by three people working at three separate desks and sharing one computer terminal at a separate table. You can change the colour scheme and add small details such as plants, pictures and lights to help create a positive working atmosphere. Use the Feng Shui top ten tips to help you.

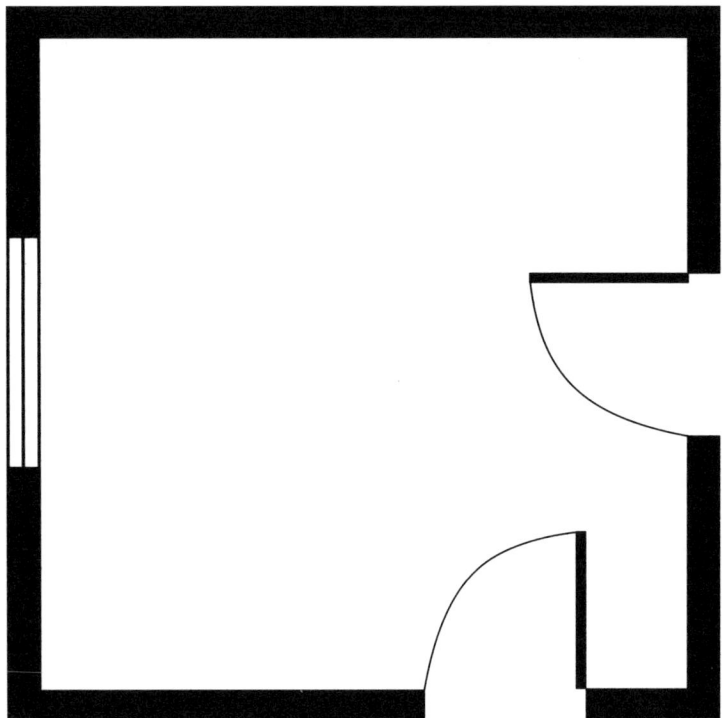

The Top Ten Tips

◇ A crowded and untidy office will cause confusion and unease in work colleagues so make sure you have enough storage space for books, paper and files.

◇ If several people share an office the desks should be arranged so that they form an octagon (or part of one) rather than having the desks in straight lines.

◇ The really important Feng Shui rule is never to sit with your back to the door when you are working.

◇ If there are two doors in your office you should position your desk so that you can see both.

◇ You can sit with your back to a window unless it faces west.

◇ Colour schemes should be kept bright and clear. White is a good working colour, while pale blue will produce a calm atmosphere. Use red only if you are sure you can cope with all the extra energy it will generate.

◇ No one should be made to sit with their back to a fellow employee nor should they have to look at large blank walls.

◇ Any dark or unused corners should be lit with lamps and any sharp corners rounded off with plants.

◇ Never put a waste bin in your money corner (the south-west corner).

◇ Try to avoid arranging furniture in straight lines or along walls.

TEACHER'S NOTES

14A Dress to kill
Russell Stannard

Type of activity
Pair work.

Aim
To practise descriptions and vocabulary of clothes.

Task
To decide how someone should dress for a job interview.

Preparation
Make one copy of the worksheet for each student.

Timing
20 minutes

Procedure
1. Give out a copy of the worksheet to each student.
2. Explain to the students that they are going to dress someone for an interview. It is a high-powered job and they should look at the clothes and select the items that they think would be most suitable.
3. Allow the students five minutes to select the clothes and **draw** them onto the model.
4. When they have finished, tell the students to complete the description below the picture.
5. Get the students to move around the class describing their pictures to each other, to form groups who have made the same – or almost the same – decisions.
6. Ask a student from each group what they chose.

INSIDE OUT *Resource Pack*

14A *Dress to kill*

Select an outfit for your model from the items on the worksheet.

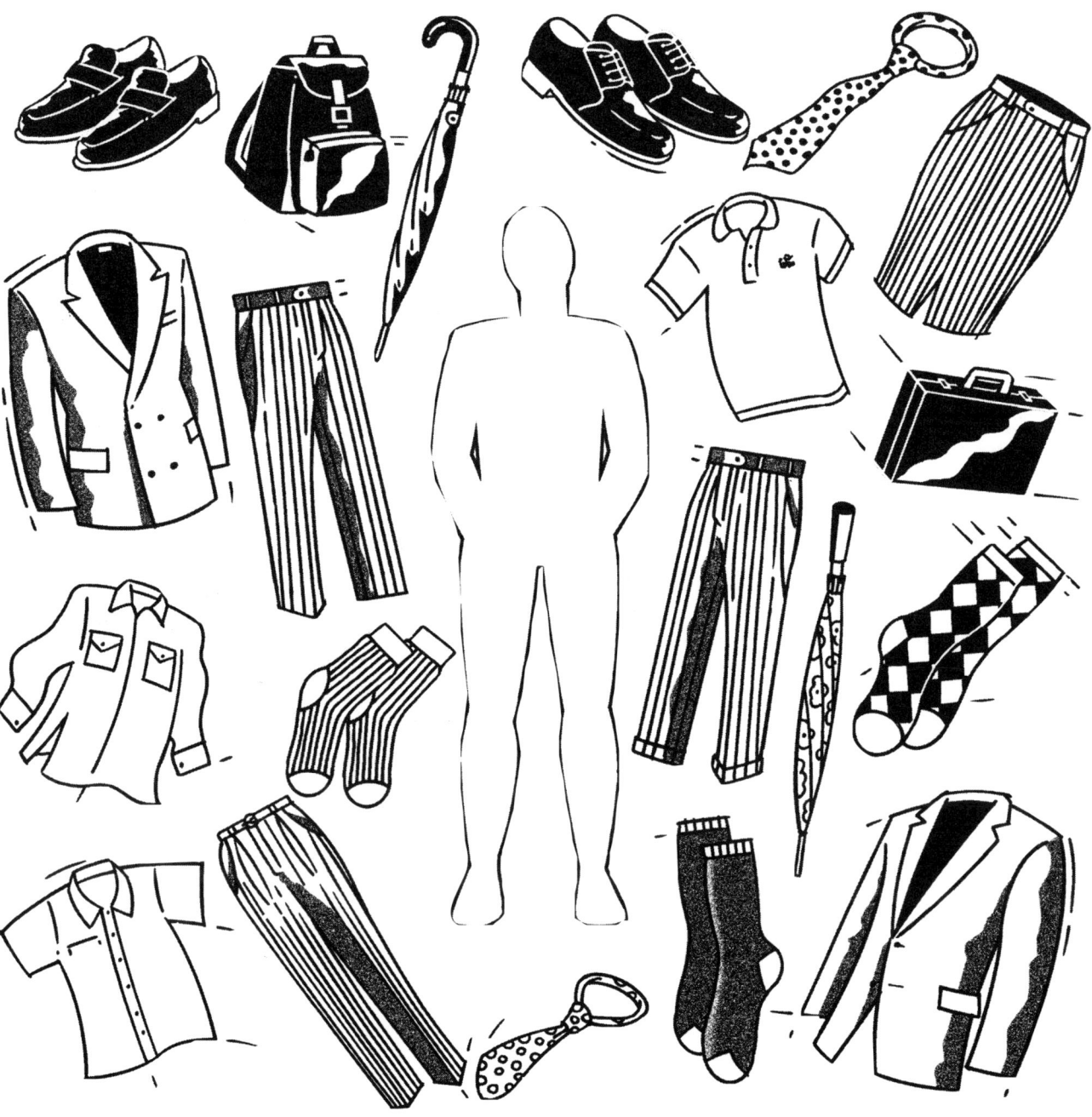

Write a description of what you've chosen. Make sure your description includes details like colours or patterns.

_____
_____
_____
_____
_____

© Sue Kay & Vaughan Jones, 2000. Published by Macmillan Publishers Limited. This sheet may be photocopied and used within the class.

Photocopiable

TEACHER'S NOTES

14B *First impressions*

Carmen Santos Maldonado

Type of activity
Writing and speaking. Individual and group work.

Aim
To practise talking about clothes and personal appearance, giving advice, negotiating, expressing opinions.

Task
To agree on a list of do's and don'ts for an interview.

Preparation
Make one copy of the worksheet for each student.

Timing
About 20 minutes.
Groups can decide what sort of job is available and write questions for the actual job interview. They can then interview two or three candidates.

Procedure
1 Tell the students that a female friend of theirs has asked for some advice for a first job interview.
2 Give each student a copy of the worksheet.
3 Ask students to read the instructions and write down their own ideas.
4 Circulate, helping with any grammar and vocabulary problems.
5 Divide the students into groups of three or four.
6 Ask the groups to agree on a common list of the most important do's and don'ts.
7 When most of the groups have finished, ask a few of them to report back to the class.

Follow up
As a whole class activity, build a common list on the board with the most popular tips suggested by all the groups.
Groups can also work on tips they would give to a male friend.

14B First impressions

A female friend of yours is going for a first job interview. She wants to know how to make the most of her appearance and how she should behave at the interview.

	DO	**DON'T**
Before the interview		
During the interview		

TEACHER'S NOTES

15A *If ...*
Jon Hird

Type of activity
Reading and writing. Whole class.

Aims
To practise using conditionals.

Task
To create a chain of conditional sentences.

Preparation
Make one copy of the worksheet and cut it up as indicated.

Timing
20 minutes

Procedure
1 Ask the students to get out a pen and a piece of paper.
2 Give each student one of the photocopied strips. Tell them to complete the sentence with anything they like as long as it makes sense and it is grammatically correct, and to write the whole sentence at the top of their piece of paper. For example, *If I were a bird, I wouldn't go to school.*
3 Ask the students to pass the sentences they have written to the next person on the left.
4 Explain what the students have to do.
 - First they should change the *main clause* of the sentence they have received to an *if clause*.
   For example, *... I wouldn't go to school* changes to *If I didn't go to school.*
 - Then they should complete the new *if clause* with a new *main clause*. For example, *If I didn't go to school, I'd miss all my friends.*
 - Then they pass the sentences on again and repeat the procedure. For example, *If I missed all my friends, I'd be unhappy.*
5 Repeat the procedure until the sentences have gone full circle.
6 Ask the students to read out their 'chains'. The class can vote for their favourite.

15A If …

If I were a bird, …

If I had magic powers, …

If I could speak perfect English, …

If I were the richest person in the world, …

If my parents hadn't met, …

If it rains tomorrow, …

If the world was going to end next week, …

If I could go anywhere in the world, …

If I had met Mahatma Gandhi, …

If I could go to the moon, …

If I were invisible, …

If I win the lottery next week, …

If aliens landed on Earth, …

If I could change sex for a day, …

If I'd been born a thousand years ago, …

If I could be any animal, …

TEACHER'S NOTES

15B *I wish*

Jon Hird

Type of activity
Writing. Mingle.

Aims
To practise the *I wish ...* structure.

Task
To complete wishes and guess who wrote them.

Preparation
Make one copy of the worksheet and cut it up as indicated.

Timing
20 minutes

Procedure
1. Give one card to each student.
2. Ask students to complete the wishes with anything that is true for them. Suggest they try to disguise their writing.
3. Collect all the cards and mix them up.
4. Ask the students to each take out one of the cards. If they have taken out their own card they should immediately replace it and take another one.
5. Ask the students to try and guess who wrote the wish. If they think they know, they should go to that person and ask them, e.g. *Do you wish you could speak Chinese?* If the guess is incorrect, they continue mingling and asking other students until they find the person who wrote the wish.
6. They should then ask why the person wrote the wish they did.
7. When all the 'wishers' have been correctly identified, the students can report back anything interesting they have learned about their classmates.
8. The procedure can be repeated with fresh wish cards being distributed.

Follow up
Don't cut up the worksheets. Give one copy to each student. The students either complete all the wishes about themselves, or they interview each other and write their partner's wishes on the worksheet.

15B *I wish ...*

I wish it was _____ _____ today.

I wish my parents would _____ _____.

I wish I was _____ _____ right now.

I wish I could speak _____ _____.

I wish I had more _____ _____.

I wish I could play _____ _____.

I wish I didn't have to _____ _____.

If only I could _____ _____ this evening.

If only I had _____ _____ when I was younger.

I wish my teachers would _____ _____.

I wish I could meet _____ _____.

I wish my country was _____ _____.

I wish my life was _____ _____.

I wish I wasn't so _____ _____.

I wish I had _____ _____ last year.

I wish I knew _____ _____.

TEACHER'S NOTES

15C *Then and now*

Ruth Sánchez García

Type of activity
Writing and speaking. Pair work.

Aim
To practise asking and answering questions.

Task
To exchange and compare personal information about the past and the present.

Preparation
Make one copy for every two students and cut the copies up as indicated.

Timing
40–45 minutes

Procedure
1 Divide the class into Student As and Student Bs and give them the relevant worksheet.
2 Allow a few minutes for them to complete the 'You' column.
3 Put the students into pairs with one Student A and one Student B in each pair.
4 Ask students to compare their answers with their partner and discuss how they have changed. Encourage students to think about the reasons why they have changed so much (or so little).
5 Circulate and monitor.
6 Ask students to compare their answers with another pair.

Follow up
Hold a discussion about the reasons why people change as they get older. Write a list on the blackboard.

15C Then and now

Student A

- Remember what you were like as a child – how you felt about things, what your attitude to life was.
- Make notes about yourself and your ideas about the topics. Then, ask your partner how he/she felt about these things. Compare your responses.
- When you've finished, discuss how your ideas have changed since then. Who has changed the most – you or your partner?

IDEAS ABOUT ...	YOU	YOUR PARTNER
1 The perfect parents		
2 The perfect partner		
3 Ideal holidays		
4 Your physical appearance		
5 The ideal job		
6 The greatest ambition in life		

✂ ....

Student B

- Remember what you were like as a child – how you felt about things, what your attitude to life was.
- Make notes about yourself and your ideas about the topics. Then, ask your partner how he/she felt about these things. Compare your responses.
- When you've finished, discuss how your ideas have changed since then. Who has changed the most – you or your partner?

IDEAS ABOUT ...	YOU	YOUR PARTNER
1 School		
2 The ideal bedroom		
3 The best way of spending money		
4 Favourite food		
5 Favourite clothes		
6 Favourite type of music/books		

© Sue Kay & Vaughan Jones, 2000. Published by Macmillan Publishers Limited. This sheet may be photocopied and used within the class.

Photocopiable

TEACHER'S NOTES

16A *How well do you know your classmates?*

Jon Hird

Type of activity
Writing, speaking. Whole class.

Aim
To practise question forms.

Task
To guess the answers to questions about your classmates and check whether or not you are correct.

Preparation
Make one copy of the worksheet for each student.

Timing
20 minutes

Procedure
1 Fold each of the worksheets as shown so that only the spaces where the students write their names are visible.
2 If possible, ask the students to sit in a circle or horseshoe.
3 Give out one worksheet to each student. They should not open out the worksheet.
4 Each student then writes their name in one of the spaces and passes the folded worksheet to the right.
5 The next student writes their name in any one of the remaining spaces, before passing it on again.
6 Continue until all the spaces have been filled. Then hand on the worksheet one more time.
7 Each student opens out the worksheet to find sixteen questions about different people, e.g. Where did <u>Anna</u> last go on holiday?
8 The students try to guess the answer to each of the questions and write this next to the question.
9 The students then mingle and ask the questions. They record with a tick (✓) or a cross (✗) whether or not they had guessed correctly.
This continues until all the questions have been asked.
10 The winner is the person who has the most correct guesses.

Follow up
In pairs, the students tell each other what they have learned.

Notes & comments
An alternative procedure is to get each student to randomly write the names of their classmates on the dotted lines. The potential problem with this, especially in bigger classes, is that some students' names may appear a lot, and others only a little if at all!
In smaller classes, fewer than sixteen, get the students to write their names in more than one slot (e.g. with a class of eight, each student fills two slots).

16A How well do you know your classmates?

↓ FOLD   FOLD ↓

What's	_____	's favourite possession?
Who in the world would	_____	most like to meet?
What's	_____	's greatest wish?
When did	_____	last have a haircut?
Which would	_____	rather be – a frog or a snake?
Where in the world would	_____	like to be right now?
How many times has	_____	been in love?
When did	_____	first kiss someone?
What's	_____	's idea of a perfect day?
Where did	_____	last go on holiday?
What will	_____	be doing at nine tonight?
How often does	_____	speak English outside class?
What's	_____	's favourite smell?
How many languages can	_____	count to ten in?
What's	_____	's favourite English word?

INSIDE OUT Resource Pack

© Sue Kay & Vaughan Jones, 2000. Published by Macmillan Publishers Limited. This sheet may be photocopied and used within the class.

Photocopiable

TEACHER'S NOTES

16B *The bear who could let it alone*

Tania Bastow and Ceri Jones

Type of activity
Problem-solving. Group or pair work.

Aim
To consolidate basic uses of prepositions and conjunctions.

Task
To read a story and replace symbols with the words they stand for.

Preparation
Make one copy of the worksheet for each pair or group of students.

Timing
15 minutes

Procedure

1. Divide the students into pairs or groups of three. Tell them that they are going to solve a puzzle.
2. Give each group one copy of the worksheet. Explain that eight words have been taken out of the text and replaced by the symbols at the bottom of the worksheet. Their task is to work out what word each symbol stands for. (If you want to add a competitive edge you can either set a time limit or say that the first group to finish is the winner.)
3. Circulate, helping with vocabulary and other problems.
4. When the first group has finished (or the time is up), stop the activity and check the answers with the whole class.

    Key:
    @ = in
    * = on
    # = of
    ✹ = by
    ? = at
    ✡ = to
    ▲ = and
    ✸ = there

16B *The bear who could let it alone*

Based on a short story
by James Thurber

@ the woods # the Far West ✷ once lived a brown bear who could take it or let it alone. @ the evenings, after work, he used ✡ go ✡ the local bar where they sold mead, a fermented drink made # honey, ▲ have just two drinks. Then he would put some money ✱ the bar ▲ say, 'See what the bears @ the back room will have,' ▲ he would go home. But finally he started drinking ✷ himself most # the day. ? the end # the night he used ✡ stagger home drunkenly, kick over the umbrella stand, knock down the lamps, ▲ stick his elbows through the windows. Then he would collapse ✱ the floor and lie ✷ until he went ✡ sleep. His wife was greatly distressed ▲ his children were very frightened.

? length the bear saw the error # his ways ▲ began ✡ reform. @ the end he became a famous teetotaller ▲ a persistent temperance lecturer. He told everybody that came ✡ his house about the awful effects # drink, ▲ he showed them how strong ▲ well he had become since he gave up drinking. ✡ demonstrate this, he used ✡ stand ✱ his head ▲ ✱ his hands ▲ turn cartwheels @ the house, kicking over the umbrella stand, knocking down the lamps, ▲ sticking his elbows through the windows. Then he used ✡ lie down ✱ the floor, tired ✷ his healthful exercise, ▲ go ✡ sleep. His wife was greatly distressed ▲ his children were very frightened.

Moral: You might as well fall flat ✱ your face as lean over too far backward.

@ =
✱ =
=
✷ =
? =
✡ =
▲ =
✷ =

TEACHING MATERIALS

7 DAY BOOK

GUILDFORD **college**

Learning Resource Centre

Please return on or before the last date shown.
No further issues or renewals if any items are overdue.

28/02/07
25 APR 2007
22 MAY 2007
 5 JUN 2007
12 JUN 2007
14 NOV 2008
24 NOV 2008
05 FEB 2009
-1 OCT 2009
26 SEP 2013

24 FEB 2014

Class: 428.24 KAY
Title: Inside Out Intermediate
Author: Kay, Sue

150236